WE'VE COME
THIS FAR
BY FAITH

Carolyn Wilde

Published by
River City Press, Inc.

①

All Scripture quotations are taken from
the King James Version of the Bible.

Excerpt from the song, "Jesus Use Me." Copyright © 1956 by
Gospel Publishing House. Used with permission. Sheet music is
available from Gospel Publishing House, Springfield, Missouri.
Order number 05-0100.

Dedication

This book was not only written to tell you about our lives, although it does do that, but the greater story of our loving God, Father, and Shepherd: the God who can be *your* God, *your* Father, *your* Shepherd.

Our testimony and our prayer are contained in these three verses from one of David's Psalms:

I waited patiently for the Lord; and he inclined unto me, and heard my cry. He brought me up also out of an horrible pit, out of the miry clay, and set my feet upon a rock, and established my goings. And he hath put a new song in my mouth, even praise unto our God: many shall see it, and fear, and shall trust in the Lord (Psalm 40:1-3).

This book is dedicated to you, with the prayer that you too will learn to trust in the Lord, "for the eyes of the Lord run to and fro throughout the whole earth, to shew himself strong in the behalf of them whose heart is perfect toward him" (II Chronicles 16:9).

Acknowledgments

I gratefully acknowledge the help and cooperation of my eight wonderful children who frequently came home from school or work and found the house in disorder with the laundry piled high, because Mom was writing a book. They would always restore order to chaos uncomplainingly, but I am sure they are as relieved as I am that this book is finished!

1

And we know that all things work together for good to them that love God, to them who are the called according to his purpose. (Romans 8:28)

It was one of those lazy, rainy Sunday afternoons in Toledo, Ohio.

Paul was on his way home with our six-year-old daughter, Kathy, thinking about his brand-new daughter he had just seen in the hospital.

All of a sudden, a car from the opposite side of the divided highway came streaking across the median, heading straight for him! The next instant there was the crash of colliding metal, the sound of breaking glass, and the two cars left the highway and came to a final stop in a field.

Paul tried to move, but the pain was excruciating. He looked over at Kathy, crying on the floor, her face covered with blood. Within seconds, he heard the wail of the ambulance, and he and his little daughter were carried back to the hospital they had just left.

How can one describe the joy and contentment of bringing a new, beautiful, healthy baby safely into the world? I was so happy. Janet Sue, our fifth child, was a perfect little bundle of joy.

"Thank you, God, thank you for another safe delivery of a child from you to us."

A nurse rushed in. "Are you Carolyn Wilde?" she asked.

"Yes."

"Your husband was just brought in to Emergency in an ambulance. He has been in a car accident!"

"Oh, God!" I breathed.

"Is he all right?" I asked her when I could find my voice.

The nurse replied, "We don't know yet. They are working on him now."

"Where is my little girl, Kathy, who was with him?"

"A girl? I didn't see any little girl in Emergency. Are you sure she was with him?"

"Yes, I'm sure!" (Was that my voice shouting?) "She just left here with him! She was in the waiting room while he visited me! He brought her to see the baby! Where is she?"

"Now calm down. I'll go see if I can find her."

Calm down?

The day was shattered, with time standing still. Was Kathy taken to a morgue? How badly was my husband hurt? Where was God?

I cried hysterically, until a new mother in the next bed called for a nurse and explained to her what was happening. "What did that nurse come and tell her for?" she muttered, and came over to the bed. "I'll find out for you," she said.

I waited for over thirty minutes. Then I got up and started for the hall to find out for myself how my husband was, and if I still had a six-year-old, blonde-haired daughter. I started to pass out, and the other mother got me back to bed. Another fifteen minutes passed, and the room telephone rang. I grabbed it, and heard Kathy's voice ask softly, "Mommy?"

I couldn't answer, for I was weeping and thanking God all at once.

"Mommy, don't cry. I'm all right. Don't cry. Where's Daddy? They took him away from me. Don't cry, Mommy."

Six years old. Kathy had just been in a car accident, her face was cut up, she had been rushed to a hospital in an ambulance, and she was worried about Daddy and comforting a nearly hysterical mother.

"Kathy, I love you. Don't worry about Daddy. I'm sure he is all right."

A few minutes later, he walked into the room. His chest had split apart and he was in agonizing pain. He couldn't stand up straight, but he insisted on walking in himself to prove to me he was okay.

A few minutes later, a kind nurse wheeled me to the waiting room to hold and hug Kathy. Her face was bandaged, but she kept saying, "Don't cry, Mommy; I'm all right."

And it was all right. It was all right that a driver, nearly senseless with a mind distorted by alcohol, had crossed a cement median and totaled our car and injured my husband and child. It was all right because Paul lay beside his bleeding daughter in that ambulance and said, "All right, God. Okay. I will serve you. I will live for you from now on. You can have my life. I won't fight you any more."

It was all right because later that same night Paul called a preacher friend of his, and asked him to pray for his chest. Roger laid hands on his chest, prayed the prayer of faith, and Paul's chest was instantly healed. All the pain was gone.

It took that dark day in our lives for Paul to say yes to following God.

But little did Paul know at that time what God would require of him as a result of that promise!

2

For whosoever will save his life shall lose it: and whosoever will lose his life for my sake shall find it. (Matthew 16:26).

I awoke with a start. It was still dark. God was gently, yet urgently, speaking within me.

Get up, and read the book of Revelation. His voice said.

I glanced at the clock on the night stand. Six o'clock in the morning.

"Read the book of Revelation at this hour?" I thought incredulously! "This is ridiculous. I always get a headache if I read the first thing in the morning!"

I had slept very little, as my five-week-old daughter had kept me up much of the night. I was just too tired to get up. I reminded the insistent voice, "I have many times read the book of Revelation, because according to Revelation 1:3, 1 am supposed to gain a blessing by reading it. But I have yet to understand any of it. It confuses me."

The voice was finally quieted, but I was left with a vague uneasiness and a feeling of guilt because of my direct disobedience to the one I claimed as Lord and Master of my life. That day I did my housework with added zeal, cleaning closets and drawers that had been neglected for weeks. But no matter what I did, I could

5

not shake off the accusing thought, "You disobeyed God this morning."

Finally in mid-afternoon, I left the contents of drawers piled on beds, walked around objects taken out of closets, and went to the living room with my Bible. Opening it to the book of Revelation, I forced myself to read each word of the twenty-two chapters.

"There," I thought, closing the Bible. "I have read it as I was instructed to, and as usual, I have received nothing from it, except a headache."

The next morning, before the sun had lit our home in Temperance, Michigan, I again woke with a start. God spoke within me, *Get up, and read the book of Revelation.*

I looked at the clock—exactly six o'clock.

"Yes, Lord," my heart answered, and I immediately arose and took my Bible to the living room. I didn't want to spend another day feeling guilty!

There was an awesome presence in the house—one I knew to be the presence of the living God. I was trembling and near tears as I found the book of Revelation. I began reading. As I read, I was startled to find the Word of God clear and easy to understand!

I ran and awoke my husband. "Come to the living room with me, honey," I said in an excited voice. "God is opening up the book of Revelation!"

Together we read that wonderful, yet terrifying, book. For eight hours, God literally opened our blinded eyes to see the truths of its pages. The presence of God filled our house. Our young children were unusually quiet. At lunch time, we hastily prepared sandwiches for them, and returned together to the Word of God.

We rejoiced as the Spirit of God explained some passages to us; we trembled as He explained others.

John, the writer of the book of Revelation, said as God gave His words to him, "It was in my mouth sweet as honey: and as soon as I had eaten it, my belly was bitter" (Revelation 10:10).

We understood that statement now. It had been so wonderful to have the very presence of the living God permeate our house that we dared only talk in hushed voices, but when the message of the book of Revelation had settled deeply inside us, it was bitter.

If we were truly living in the end time, when many of the prophecies of the book of Revelation were to be fulfilled, our goals and aims in life were meaningless. Only one thing was important: Were our names written in the Lamb's Book of Life?

The beautiful ranch home we were buying would someday be gone. Our possessions would be burned with fire. The social status we sought for in our community, the popularity we hoped for, were both worthless. Indeed, our endless quest for worldly possessions was futile, even if we were successful in attaining the goals we had set for ourselves.

I had heard Paul say as he spoke before a room full of sales people, "Someday, I will be driving a Rolls Royce!"

What concerned us now was that someday we would be standing before the throne of God when He judges His creation. What would our possessions mean to us then?

7

We quaked inside. We were obsessed with materialistic goals in this life. Our one aim was to possess all the riches this world could offer. Oh, we had glibly quoted in the past, "For what shall it profit a man if he shall gain the whole world and lose his own soul," but we hadn't really thought it applied to us. Hadn't we professed Christ as our personal Savior and Lord at an early age? Didn't we attend church two or three times a week? Weren't we even serving Him with our musical talents?

But the bitter truth upset us. A godless dictator would one day rule this earth.

To refuse to serve this world ruler would be to forfeit the right to buy and sell.

If we were ever actually faced with making a decision between serving a world ruler and Jesus Christ, whom we professed to love and serve, how could we possibly serve Jesus? If we could neither buy nor sell, we would starve to death! Our children, entrusted to our care, could starve to death before our very eyes! We would lose every single possession we had spent years to obtain! Jesus hardly meant enough to our everyday lives to make that kind of commitment to Him.

We knew the disciples and the early Christians were martyred for Jesus Christ. And we know Christians under Communistic rule today are suffering and giving their lives for Christ. But we didn't want any part of it! And yet every time we picked up our Bibles, it would open right up to verses like these:

If we suffer, we shall also reign with him: if we deny him, he also will deny us (II Timothy 2:12).

*In the world ye shall have tribulation: but
be of good cheer; I have overcome the world*
(John 16:33).

*We must through much tribulation enter
into the kingdom of God* (Acts 14:22).

*Yea, and all that will live godly in Christ
Jesus shall suffer persecution* (11 Timothy 3:12).

Even Christians in America, Lord?

As for us, we had never made the kind of commitment
to Christ that included suffering anything. We just
wanted to go to heaven when we died. It hadn't occurred
to us that Christ required more of us than attending
church on Sundays!

Now we could see why John had relished the pleasant
taste of the book as he ate it—but in his stomach, it was
bitter.

There was yet another source of bitterness stirring
within us. Within our hearts, we knew Paul was being
called to preach the gospel. We knew God wanted him
also to warn backslidden, flippant, unconcerned
children of God that we had all better make a
wholehearted commitment to Jesus Christ, in light of the
nearness of the closing of time and the coming persecution of God's people.

Paul literally paced the floor and raved for days. "I
won't! I refuse even to believe all this myself, much less
preach it!"

As surely as he knew in his heart the book of Revelation was true, he also knew that we ourselves were not ready

9

to face any persecution for the sake of Jesus. Our commitment to Christ was only for the keeping of our souls, and did not include the giving of our bodies! Now God was demanding a full commitment from us.

We read in God's Word:

> *I beseech you therefore, brethren, by the mercies of God, that ye present your bodies a living sacrifice, holy, acceptable unto God, which is your reasonable service* (Romans 12:1).

> *What? know ye not that your body is the temple of the Holy Ghost which is in you, which ye have of God, and ye are not your own? For ye are bought with a price: therefore glorify God in your body, and in your spirit, which are God's* (I Corinthians 6:19-20).

We pondered these Scriptures for weeks. What a decision it was for us to relinquish control of our lives to God. If we had understood then the abundant life of peace and blessing God gives to those who fully serve Him, our decision would have been easy.

3

For ye see your calling, brethren, how that not many wise men after the flesh, not many mighty, not many noble, are called: but God hath chosen the foolish things of the world to confound the wise; and God hath chosen the weak things of the world to confound the things which are mighty; and base things of the world, and things which are despised, hath God chosen, yea, and things which are not, to bring to nought things that are: that no flesh should glory in his presence. (I Corinthians 1:26-29)

Questions poured into our minds even faster than words could form them.

"Why us, Lord? We have five little children. You know we have just failed miserably in a business, and are deeply in debt to many people. You must realize Paul has no seminary training. It is true we might have to die for you someday. Okay, we accept that. But we want you to know that just because we think we are becoming willing to die for you, does not mean we are going to be able to live for you!"

Paul thrust himself wholeheartedly into making music for the Lord. He sang and played the saxophone every chance he could get. He emceed a live, hour-long "Sunday Evening Sing-Along" on a gospel radio station. We went as far as being booked with the Speer Family for a gospel concert. But the week before the concert,

God spoke to Paul's heart that he was not to take part in it. Paul was greatly disappointed, but had enough fear of God that he canceled his part in the concert.

We simply attended the concert; our pianist took our place and played some special numbers. Why wouldn't God settle for our singing and some good saxophone playing? We were doing it for Him! But Paul knew in his heart that God wanted him to preach. During the concert, he sunk lower in his seat rebelling against God's plan for his life and reminded God of the many reasons why he couldn't obey His call. He fought the idea of God taking control of our lives.

Days followed days—days of misery, unhappiness, unrest, and confusion. Our minds were continually trying to talk our hearts out of doing what we were supposed to do. We simply refused to turn our lives over to God. We wanted Him to be our Savior, but we did not want Him to be our Lord.

We were troubled, in turmoil, and couldn't even sleep nights, as we continued to resist the call of God on our lives. Our debts, lack of seminary training, and five small children to provide for, seemed to be insurmountable obstacles in the path we knew God was asking us to walk. And yet we felt our lives had lost all meaning and purpose, as we were living only for the trivialities—and even the necessities—of this life.

Then one day we saw the advertisement of a coming revival meeting in the Toledo Sports Arena. It mentioned that the speaker, Billy Walker, Jr., had been a Southern Baptist child preacher. Since I had been raised in a Baptist church, we decided to attend the meeting.

Then the fight began—an argument between my husband and me over some trivial thing—a spiritual fight to get to that meeting. It was as if Satan had sent a whole crew of devils into our home to keep us from going. Everything went wrong. (Since we had five children, and the oldest one was only six years old, there was much that could go wrong!)

We finally gave up and decided not to go. (We have learned since that night not to give up so easily. If Satan is battling to keep you home from church, determine to go, no matter what, for God has a special blessing in store for you!)

A few minutes after our decision to stay home, friends of ours knocked on our door.

"Hey," Roger said, "did you see this announcement of a revival meeting? Let's go!"

We knew we would be late, but we went anyway. All the way there, I silently prayed, "Father, do you really want us in the ministry? Do you really want my husband to preach? Are you really asking us to work for you full-time? If you really are, Lord, in Jesus' name, I ask you to have this Southern Baptist preacher we are going to hear tonight tell Paul that you want him to preach—and have him tell him right in the middle of his sermon!"

You probably wonder why I prayed a prayer like that. My idea of the ministry was that Paul would begin to travel and preach—something like the circuit riding preachers of the past. And I was convinced that our children and I were about to lose a husband and father to God. I didn't like the idea at all. I loved my husband

13

and had specific ideas about home life—and they all included him!

I thought I'd prayed a safe enough prayer, as I had never seen a Baptist preacher stop in the middle of a sermon to tell someone that God was calling him to preach!

We sat towards the front of that arena, and watched Billy Walker preach. He was jumping around and hollering. We had never seen a preacher like him. I was embarrassed, because Paul didn't like him at all, but we were too far up front to leave, so Paul sat with his arms folded and glared at him. Billy just kept waving his arms and shouting.

Then he stopped.

"There is someone in this congregation by the name of Paul. Please stand up. God has a word for you."

I stole a glance at my husband. "Lots of Pauls here," he mumbled, but I noticed he was a shade whiter!

"Paul, please stand up. I cannot continue my sermon until I deliver this message God has for you."

Paul leaned over towards me. "Feel my chest," he whispered. "My heart is thudding. I think I'm having a heart attack." Now he was several shades whiter than I was.

Billy walked over to our side of the auditorium and walked back and forth in front of us. Then his finger pointed straight at my husband. "You! Stand up!"

Paul stood up—all six feet, two inches of him. (Billy was about five and a half feet tall.)

Paul was shaking as Billy delivered the message God had for him. He told Paul that God wanted to use him, but he was still worrying too much about what people thought of him. He told him other things about his life. They were all true.

While Billy was talking to my husband, I gave in completely to the Lord. "All right," I prayed. "Even if my husband travels, I will stay home willingly, so the gospel message can be preached. And even if I have to leave my children in your care and go with Paul, I will do it for you. You take control of our lives and home from now on. We give our whole family to you, and entrust our children, our home, our marriage—everything to your care."

That too was a promise God would remind me of many times—a promise I had made to Him, and that He would require me to keep.

4

And the Lord God said, It is not good that the man should be alone; I will make him an help meet for him. (Genesis 2:18)

That promise to God was not made lightly. Shortly before I made it, Paul was "Mr. Enthusiasm!" for a lighting division of Lear-Seigler, Inc. He had traveled from state to state training and inspiring sales managers and introducing new products to them. He had been a speaker at many sales conventions.

And he had not been home much at all. Most weeks we had only our weekends together. Each Monday morning he would leave, and I knew I wouldn't see him again until Saturday morning or afternoon.

I didn't cope too well without him, to say the least. It seemed that every time he left, something would break: the car, washing machine, sewing machine, iron, toaster, refrigerator, stove—always something.

The teacher who gave me my aptitude test during my final year of high school advised me, "Carolyn, you would do well in social work or as a bookkeeper. But if you decide to do bookkeeping, don't ever attempt to change a typewriter ribbon. You are the *stupidest* person I have ever seen, when it comes to mechanics!"

One late afternoon, there was a thunderstorm. All of a sudden, the lights went out, the radio died, and sparks began flying out of the fuse box. The crackling and sparks stopped, and smoke poured from the box. I noticed our porch light was the only light still on. I turned off the back burner of the electric stove I had been cooking on. The porch light went off! I turned on the burner again. The light went back on! Sure enough, the control to the back burner was controlling the porch light!

The furnace quit. I waited until the temperature got down to 54 degrees, and then went to the telephone. It was dead.

I packed the kids in the car to go telephone some friends for help. Before I got half a block, the car sputtered and stopped. By then I was furious at Paul. He was probably in a fancy, warm restaurant someplace, basking in the praise of salesmen, after giving his speech about lights—of which I had only one on the front porch! And it was controlled by my electric stove!

I walked to a gas station and called our friends whom I had just recently become acquainted with.

Twila answered. "Yes, Carolyn," she said," is something wrong?"

"Yes, just a few little things. Could you come over?"

Roger and Twila came over. They gave up on the car, electricity, furnace, and telephone, and packed us into their car and took us home with them.

Later that night, Paul called from Denver. "Could you check and see if my family is all right? I can't reach them, and I know Carolyn wouldn't have gone!"

I gritted my teeth and took the phone. He said, "What are you doing there? Listen, the president of the company asked if I would go to California from here and then on to some other states. It would be about a three week tour... Are you still there?"

He found out I was still there! "Wait," he interrupted my tirade, "I just wanted to tell you I told him no. He is upset, but I couldn't leave you and the children that long!"

He flew in two days later on Saturday. The electricity and car were still not fixed, and we had slept on an apartment couch and floor. Our friends had graciously taken me to the airport to meet my husband. We were late, and I didn't care. But he did. We argued, but when we got home, he took me in his arms and said, "I've married you and left you. I have five children, and I have left them too. All for money and power and prestige. I am going to quit traveling and take care of my family."

I loved him so very much. Even though the world of business had been trying to separate us, we still loved each other deeply. There was never a doubt in my mind that he was the man God had chosen to be my husband, and that God had made me to be a help to him.

I had been engaged to marry someone else, but God had intervened. One Sunday evening, in a little Assembly of God church in Petoskey, Michigan, God spoke to me to break the engagement because it was not His will for my life. I fought with the Lord through the entire sermon, and at the end of it, I went to the altar to pray. "Lord, don't you want me to get married? You know there is a shortage of Christian guys in this town!" But I couldn't get any peace until I prayed, "All right. If you will help me write to my fiance and break this engagement, I will do it tonight."

I felt a load fall off me, and even though I could not understand God's leading, I felt peace about it. I got to my feet, and my twelve-year-old brother was there.

"Your brother is out in front of the church, and he wants to see you," he said.

"My brother? What are you talking about?"

"All I know," he answered, "is that there is some dude out there who says he wants to talk to Carolyn Crawford, and he says he is your brother. I've never seen him before!"

I went outside, and there stood Paul. I vaguely knew him as the guy who had dated some of my girlfriends and who played his saxophone in youth rallies sometimes.

"Hi," he said. "I have driven fifteen miles in a blizzard to ask you to go have a Coke with me at Wimpy's."

"I am engaged," I said.

"Yeah, I know. I am going steady," he answered.

I looked up at him. He was big, strong, handsome, and had kind eyes, and my heart sort of turned over. Was this God's reason for my broken engagement? But I hadn't broken it yet. "We'd better not," I answered him.

"Look, I was sitting in church in Alanson, and all I could think about was that I should come here and talk to you. I didn't have enough money for gas, so I talked my cousin into coming with me, so I would have someone to chip in on gas. Let's just go and talk for a while."

I looked in his car. Sure enough, his cousin was there.

"All right," I said. "We'll go to Wimpy's. You take your cousin and your car. I will take my cousin, my brother, and my car and meet you there!"

A few minutes later, I introduced my brother to him. Paul stared at Karl. "That's the kid I sent ...."

"Yes, this is my brother—the one you sent to tell me that my 'brother' wanted to see me!"

"Well, I am your brother in the Lord," Paul told me later.

Four months after that evening we were married. Neither one of us have ever doubted that God meant us to be together. Paul had prayed for a Christian wife. And I had broken an engagement to obey God. He had blessed us abundantly for that, and had given us a beautiful marriage. Christian people would not find themselves involved in divorce if they allowed God to choose their marriage partners.

Paul walked into the president's office at the lighting company and said, "I quit. I want to live with my wife and children full-time."

"Are you crazy? You have unlimited opportunities here in our company. You could go to the top!"

But Paul quit, and we were happy because we were together.

And now, God was asking if I was willing to be separated again to work for Him. And this time, because of a love for God and a desire to please Him, my answer was yes.

So far, after over twenty years of working for God, we have only been separated once during a weekend revival meeting. God has graciously kept us working side by side for Him. I believe though, that God wanted our love for Him to surpass the love we had for each other. We had to become *willing* to be separated from each other, before God could use us effectively as His servants.

I dedicated my life to God that night in the revival meeting. After that meeting, Paul began to spend hours each day listening to one song over and over again on our record player:

Jesus, use me.
Please Lord, don't refuse me.
Surely there's a work that I can do.
And even though it's humble,
Help my will to crumble.
Though the cost be great,
I'll work for You.

Hundreds of times he sang that song along with the record. "Help my will to crumble" became the prayer of his life, until God answered that cry, and he could honestly say, "Though the cost be great, I'll work for you."

Paul was in the basement of our home, when God's will replaced his own.

In the room that had been used as a snack bar, he laid before God and wept so hard, his nose began to bleed. He knew what God was demanding. Total obedience. His entire life. Giving up every ambition, every goal. Becoming willing to live and raise his family in poverty.

Giving everything he had and ever hoped to have to the One who gave His life for him. God was demanding that Paul keep the promise he had made to Him in the ambulance that rainy Sunday.

Finally, laying in a pool of blood and tears, the old selfish will and self-centered desires died, and only the desire to be used of God remained.

Some Christians may die to self easily and suddenly, but Paul's was a slow, painful death. Some never crucify that old self at all and try to follow two lords all their lives—self and Jesus. God's Word says, "They that are Christ's have crucified the flesh with the affections and lusts" (Galatians 5:24).

It was an agonizing death to self but Paul came up from that basement a different person.

What a change from the past few weeks! The sun shone again! We could smile and laugh! Our outlook on life was bright and optimistic. We could finally say with the apostle Paul, "Christ shall be magnified in my body, whether it be by life, or by death. For to me to live is Christ, and to die is gain" (Philippians 1:20-21). Faith replaced fear, as we rested securely in the loving care of our heavenly Father and gave control of our lives to Him.

But there was another problem. "God," I prayed, "we are in a big financial mess. You said in your Word that we could speak to a mountain in the name of Jesus, and it would be removed. Well, our bills are a mountain that needs to be removed."

"You also said to cast all our cares upon you, because you care for us. All must include this mountain of bills.

By faith, I am going to turn these bills over to you. Here they are!"

God didn't immediately dispatch an angel to Temperance, Michigan with a heavenly check to pay our debts. But He gave me something even more valuable. He replaced my burden with a beautiful peace.

That evening, God took away all the bitterness toward people that had been festering inside me, and replaced it with love, understanding, and forgiveness.

I had been bitter toward those who had been partially responsible for our business failure. I was bitter toward a man who had failed to keep his word to us, and had cheated us out of enough money to pay every debt we owed. All that bitterness had done exactly what God's Word said it would do in Hebrews 12:15. It had defiled me, and robbed me of joy and peace that should have been mine as a child of God.

I had been raised by debt-free parents, without a single care or worry in life. My folks readily supplied my every need. Because of my carefree life, I had somehow decided that anyone who had debts was either lazy or ignorant. I remember the day my mother told me that we had what we had because God blessed the labors of my hard-working father. She said it could all be taken away from us overnight, if God allowed Satan to strip away our blessings as he had Job's. But I still believed that anyone who was burdened down with debts was either lazy or ignorant. Now we were deeply in debt, and Paul was neither lazy nor ignorant. God taught me through bitter experience that circumstances in life cause debts too.

What good would I have been to God with my snobbish attitude toward those who were deeply in debt? In one of Jesus' first sermons, He stood in the Jewish synagogue and said, "The Spirit of the Lord is upon me, because he hath anointed me to preach the gospel to the poor" (Luke 4:18).

For the first time, I could honestly pray, "Lord, thank you for allowing us to fail miserably. Thank you for our debts. They have made me a better person. I still want you to pay them but I know now it has all worked for good in our lives."

But I still couldn't see how we could possibly begin to serve the Lord full-time when we had bills to pay and five children to feed and clothe.

I had a lot to learn about God, and His ability to lead and feed His sheep!

5

All things are of God, who hath reconciled us to himself by Jesus Christ, and hath given to us the ministry of reconciliation. Now then we are ambassadors for Christ.
(II Corinthians 5:18, 20)

God had called us to work for Him and He had broken our stubborn wills. We had finally said yes to His call. Now what were we supposed to do?

Every day, Paul went out selling with the song in his heart, "Jesus, Use Me."

And Jesus did.

He was in a hardware store one afternoon shortly after lunch. He had gone in to sell material goods, but instead found himself offering free salvation to the owner of the store.

"I know you believe Jesus Christ is the Son of God," he told the elderly gentleman. "But the devil believes that, and God prepared hell for him. You see, there is more to salvation than just believing Jesus is the Son of God. That is just the first step to being born again. God's Word says we must 'believe on the *Lord* Jesus Christ' (Acts 16:31) to be saved. Lord means Master. Jesus Christ must become your Savior, as well as your Master. You must become His servant.

"Do you know how to be really born again?"

25

"No," the man answered. "I don't understand what that means."

Paul explained, "When your father placed a seed in your mother and she conceived, your physical life began. In order for spiritual life to begin for you, you must become the fertile womb in which God can implant His seed. But you have sinned, and you are too dirty a vessel for God to place His seed into. He is holy. Man is dirty. But the good news is that you can become clean enough for God to come into. Do you know how?"

"No, I don't. I've gone to church for years, but I have never heard about this!"

"The blood Jesus shed when He gave His life for you on the cross can cleanse you from all your sins. The blood of Jesus can wash your sins away, and in God's sight, you can be just as if you had never sinned. God will not only forgive you of your sin, He will cleanse you and He will even *forget* your sins!"

"How can I have this?" the man asked.

Paul said, "The blood is applied to you when you repent of your sins and ask God to save you, and invite Jesus to come and live within you."

The gentleman interrupted with, "I was always taught we should just live a good life and not treat anybody wrong, and then I would stand as good a chance as anybody of going to heaven."

Paul asked him, "Do you think Jesus would have come down from heaven and suffered a beating and agonizing death on a cross at the hands of His own creation, if you could have gone to heaven without His dying for you? You cannot earn your salvation! Jesus earned

26

it for you. Accept the blood He shed, and trust Him alone for your salvation!"

"When you repent, He washes all your sins away with His blood, then the Holy God comes to dwell within you, and spiritually you are born. Jesus alone gives you spiritual life, and God said, 'Except a man be born again, he cannot see the kingdom of God.' Do you want to be born again?"

"Just a minute," the man said. He walked into the back room and came back with some keys. He then went to a desk and picked up a sign. He went to the front of his store, hung the "Closed" sign in his window, and locked potential customers out of his store.

Then he came back and said, "There! If I am going to be doing business with God, I don't want to be trying to do business with people at the same time."

He knelt on the floor, and in the childlike faith God said it would take to receive Jesus Christ, he asked for forgiveness of his sins. He thanked Jesus for dying to save him, and with tears streaming down his face, he asked Him to come and live in his heart. The Bible says that the angels rejoice when one sinner repents (Luke 15:10), and two men in a hardware store joined their heavenly chorus that afternoon.

Paul came home. "Did you sell anything?" I asked as I greeted him. Our cupboards were nearly empty, and I had planned to go grocery shopping.

"No," he answered, grinning, "but a man was saved today!"

Paul was transformed. He would leave in the mornings intending to have a prosperous day selling, but when he met potential customers, he was more

27

concerned about their lost souls than about his lost sales. He led people to the Lord nearly every day—service station managers and workers, owners of stores, body shop workers, purchasing agents—people from all walks of life.

I was rejoicing with him as the Lord used him to bring lost people to salvation. But I was upset too, because his sales had dropped considerably.

"I can't think about these things anymore, Carolyn," he said to me one night. "Sales aren't important. Christ is. Lost souls are. I just can't get excited about anything but leading people to Christ!"

"But what about our bills? Groceries? Clothes? We need money to exist in this life! We can't just live for heaven!" I looked at him. "Can we?"

I went to the Bible for help. It seemed that the sixth chapter of Matthew had been written just for me to read that night:

> *Therefore I say unto you, Take no thought for your life, what ye shall eat, or what ye shall drink; nor yet for your body, what ye shall put on. Is not the life more than meat, and the body than raiment?*
>
> *Behold the fowls of the air: for they sow not, neither do they reap, nor gather into barns; yet your heavenly Father feedeth them. Are ye not much better than they?*
>
> *Which of you by taking thought can add one cubit unto his stature?*

And why take ye thought for raiment?
Consider the lilies of the field, how they grow;
they toil not, neither do they spin:
And yet I say unto you, That even Solomon
in all his glory was not arrayed like one of these.

Wherefore, if God clothe the grass of the
field, which today is, and tomorrow is cast into
the oven, shall he much more clothe you, O
ye of little faith?

Therefore take no thought saying, What shall
we eat? or, What shall we drink? or, Wherewithal
shall we be clothed?

(For after all these things do the Gentiles
seek:) for your heavenly Father knoweth that ye
have need of all these things.

But seek ye first the kingdom of God, and his
righteousness; and all these things shall be
added unto you (Matthew 6:25-33).

"O God," I prayed, "that is what Paul is doing. He is seeking you first, before anything else. So are you really going to take care of *us*, as your Word says you are? Now—in this day and age—does what you said two-thousand years ago work? Because if you are really going to take care of us, we need some money to keep our family going."

We attended a revival meeting. The evangelist asked the people to bring their offerings to the front of the auditorium. I watched Paul go and put every single cent he had into the offering plate.

"How are we going to even buy gas for the car tomorrow?" I thought. On the way back to his seat, Paul was stopped by a man who reached out for him as he went by.

"Aren't you a lighting salesman?" he asked. "I own a car dealership. Will you stop by tomorrow? I am going to change the lighting in my showroom."

Paul had given probably less than twenty dollars to one of God's servants. But it was all he had, and God showed us that evening that He always blesses that kind of giving. Before he even returned to his seat God had given him his next day's sales, and because Paul had his own lighting business now, the profit was hundreds of dollars.

We were just beginning to find out that God does take care of His children who seek Him first.

6

*When thou makest a dinner or a supper, call not thy
friends, nor thy brethren, neither thy kinsmen, nor thy
rich neighbours; lest they also bid thee again, and a
recompence be made thee. But when thou makest a feast,
call the poor, the maimed, the lame, the blind: And thou
shalt be blessed; for they cannot recompense thee: for
thou shalt be recompensed at the resurrection of the just.*
(Luke 14:12-14)

*If a brother or sister be naked, and destitute of
daily food, And one of you say unto them, Depart in
peace, be ye warmed and filled; notwithstanding ye give
them not those things which are needful to the body,-
what doth it profit?* *(James 2:15-16)*

One day we received a call from a local church. "We
have a group from our church going to the Toledo
Rescue Mission Monday evening. Will you go along
with us and provide the music?"

"We would love to," we answered.

Monday evening the group met at our neighbor's home
and went to the mission from there. The women were
dressed in their finest; some had fur coats and carried
expensive leather purses. It seemed rather pretentious to
dress like that to go to a mission and try to reach men
who had literally nothing. But by the time the evening
was over, we doubted whether they were trying to

reach these men at all. It seemed more as if they were just trying to chalk up another good deed in heaven!

The couples filed in, the women exchanging looks when they passed one of the dirty alcoholics.

They finally found a section of pews where they could all sit together, away from all the men attending the mission.

Five minutes before the service started, all the men from the church filed into a back room to ask God's blessing on the service. Then they filed back in, and the service began. We sang, I played the piano, and Paul played the saxophone. A man gave a short, pious, uninteresting sermon, and the meeting was over for another month for this particular group.

On our way out, Paul went over to shake hands with a homeless man. The Christians looked at him aghast, and hurried from the building.

"Fresh air," they said, as they closed the door on that little mission and its miserable occupants.

Later they all met back at our neighbor's house for a feast. They scrubbed their hands vigorously before eating, because some had actually touched the hymnals at the mission! Women were brushing invisible dirt from their clothes, and finally we all sat down to eat.

Just after grace, Paul said, "I wonder what those poor men at the mission are eating tonight?" His remark put a damper on the meal and the atmosphere became rather tense, so we ate a few bites and went home.

Paul was upset. "Nobody wanted to get dirty! They completely ignored the men they were supposed to be ministering to! They wouldn't even shake their hands or do more than nod to them as they hurried past," he raved. "And then they went home to eat fancy dishes it probably took two days to prepare. I wonder what those men at the mission were eating?"

Paul had to find out. He went down to the mission the next day.

"What did you give the men to eat last night?" he asked.

"What we always give them," the man in charge of the mission answered tiredly. "Watered-down soup and bread."

"Can I see it?"

"I guess so. Come on down to the basement where the men eat. You see, none of them would come to the church services we have here every night, but they can't eat unless they attend the church service first. So they come just to get a free meal. We just barely get by as far as food goes. Here is the soup. We get bread from the day-old bakery. There is no butter or oleo for the bread."

He opened the simmering kettle and Paul stared in. It looked like murky water. He thought about the banquet that was laid before the church group the evening before, and he felt sick.

"Listen, do you have any free nights during the week when a friend of mine and I could take the mission?" he asked.

"Just Sunday nights," was the answer. "Nobody will come then, because that is their church night."

"Put me down. And don't fix any soup that night or get any bread. We will bring the food, and we will come down to the basement after the service and serve it to the men. We will see you this Sunday."

That was the first weekend of many that Twila and I spent cooking. We took a full-course meal down to the men, and after the service, Paul donned a big white apron, and served the meal. We all went downstairs and ate with them and visited with them. Those men really ate, and the next Sunday, there was a bigger crowd. After a few weeks, word got around about a real feast on Sunday nights, and men came from all over Toledo. We found out something about those men while eating with them after the services. We met doctors, lawyers —men from all walks of life whose lives had been ruined by turning to alcohol to forget business failures, bad marriages, or their own shortcomings. Some of them came only for a good meal but found a new hope and a new life in Jesus Christ.

One big man came sobbing to the altar during the altar call, and cried out to Christ to save him and help him. He had been a deacon in a Baptist church in Massachusetts. He had nine children. He left Toledo that same evening to go back to his family and take his responsibility of being a husband and father once again.

Paul insisted on stopping on the way to the mission one Sunday to buy the men ice cream to go along with the cakes we had baked. "Ice cream? Why do they have to have ice cream?" I questioned, thinking about our dwindling funds again.

"Well," he answered, "I love ice cream. Some of them probably do too."

He was right. They were as excited as little children when he served them ice cream. The next Sunday evening, the mission was packed!

We took one young man home with us for a few weeks. It was so hard for them to get back on their feet again physically and spiritually. A bus picked up men in Toledo then, and took them to a place that needed cheap labor. The men would work for a day, be given a check for their labor, and then were taken back to the city. The problem was that no one would cash their checks but a friendly barkeeper. And he would only do it if they would buy something from him. It was a temptation few alcoholics could resist. So we took one man home to get him away from the environment. After he had stayed in our home for nearly a week, he told us how his life got off to a wrong start. He had shot and killed his sister when they were both teenagers.

Paul and I exchanged looks. And he was staying with us and our five children? We hastily questioned our own sanity. We had a murderer living with us! Then the peace of God settled over us, and we looked at our guest. He was hardly anyone to fear. He was a young man, but aged and broken by guilt and the alcohol he had consumed to forget his sin. Thank God he had Jesus now as His loving, compassionate Savior and Friend who had given His own life's blood to save this broken man.

One morning, we heard on the local newscast that a "skid row bum" had frozen to death on the sidewalk, huddled close to a building for warmth and shelter.

"I can't sell today," Paul said. "Get ready, and we will go try to find some warm clothes for the guys at the mission." We came home much later with a car so full

35

we could hardly sit in it. We had found a used clothing store that had given us many clothes and charged very little for others. Sunday evening, after the dinner, Paul had the men line up. By the time he finished outfitting them, one could hardly tell them apart from the rest of us! They left the mission that night, all dressed up in topcoats, scarves, hats—looking like dudes!

The following Sunday, most of them came back looking just as they had before Paul gave them clothes —dressed in their old tattered shirts, no coats, no hats. "Where are your warm clothes?" Paul almost shouted.

"Sold 'em," some mumbled, not meeting his eyes. They had sold their clothing for another bottle of body destroying, soul-damning liquor. The manager of the mission told us, "Those men get handouts by begging on the streets. They wouldn't be able to get money, looking like they did. They were dressed better than the people they were begging from!"

Mission work was sometimes discouraging.

We had always provided the music for the services, and Roger had preached, with good results. But one week, Paul told Roger, "I have something to say to the men this week." He preached his first sermon to those outcasts of society.

He took Peter's words, spoken to a beggar two-thousand years earlier, and applied them to the beggars of Toledo, Ohio: "Silver and gold have I none, but such as I have give I thee. In the name of Jesus Christ of Nazareth, rise up and walk" (Acts 3:6).

It was Paul's first real sermon. A couple of the men slept through it—one man fell off the pew.

And some men took heed to it and were saved that night. They knelt at the altar, seeking their Creator, and asking Him to be their Savior. No one but Jesus, whom we served, could pick up these broken men and help them to walk in this life without the crutch of alcohol. What a privilege it is to work for one who can solve every problem and meet every need; one who has love, compassion and time for every person who comes to Him.

One Sunday we could not find a baby sitter for our children. "What should we do?" I asked Paul.

"We will take the kids with us!" he answered.

"To the mission? On skid row?"

"The Lord will protect them. Get them ready."

We walked in with our five little children. Before the music started that evening, many of the men were weeping. Our children reminded them of children they had left fatherless. Dennis, who was four then, loved one big black man in particular. He snuggled up to him while I went to play the piano. After the service, Dennis followed him everywhere, and was really sad when we had to leave.

We took our children to the mission often after that. It was not only good for them to be involved in helping people in need, but our children stirred memories of the father's own abandoned children, showing them what their lives could have been, had they followed Jesus, instead of committing their lives to alcohol.

Paul also became involved in radio work. One afternoon, he had just finished a live program in Detroit, discussing Bible prophecy with a converted Jew who was a dynamic evangelist. The telephone rang in the radio studio after the program. A weeping woman asked

Elliot and Paul if they would come to her home and help her and her family. They went immediately to her house, and found a lovely Catholic family in need of spiritual help. Before the evening was over, the husband, wife, and their children knelt in the dining room and gave their lives and entrusted their souls, not to a religion, but to Jesus Christ.

Our days and evenings were spent in some way working in our Lord's harvest field. On Sunday mornings, we led a junior church service in a Methodist church. It was one of those positions nobody wanted to fill, but we had a great time. It sometimes took some pretty drastic measures to hold the attention of scores of children —especially if the preacher held the regular service overtime! So Paul began dramatizing Bible events. One morning he was Goliath. He picked a little David from the group of kids, and the show was on.

After Goliath roared at David for a while, David finally went through the motions of killing the giant. The giant fell with a crash and continued to lay there. I rushed over to see if he was unconscious, disgusted because he had overdone the crash and I was sure I would find his head split open. He was all right, but admitted he had overdone things a little and was momentarily stunned. Serving the Lord was anything but dull!

We knew God was calling Paul to preach in churches, but during this time, we served Him where we were, waiting on Him for guidance and praying for direction. The answer came in two dreams.

7

The sheep hear his voice: and he calleth his own sheep by name, and leadeth them out. And when he putteth forth his own sheep, he goeth before them, and the sheep follow him: for they know his voice. (John 10:3-4)

Paul had a vivid dream one night that we were to move to Hart, Michigan.

I had never been there. Paul had been born in Hart, but his parents had moved from there when he was about four years old.

We started to Hart the next day, praying, "Lord, is this your voice? Is this really where you want us to go?"

We stayed overnight in Lansing on our way to Hart, and that night Paul had the identical dream the second time—move to Hart.

We prayed that God would confirm the dreams by opening the door for us to live there.

It was March. I had forgotten since living in the Toledo area what Michigan winters are like, and I had to buy boots to get around the town.

"God," we prayed, "if you are leading us here, you have to have a house for us to rent."

"Impossible!" was the realtor's response to our request for a house to rent for a family of seven. "There just aren't any."

"Well," Paul answered, "We will go eat lunch, and come back this afternoon to see if you have thought of one."

We returned to his office. "There still aren't any," he said curtly. "Sorry."

We stayed in his office. The realtor was trying to dismiss us, but Paul wasn't taking his hints, and I was getting embarrassed. "Are you sure?" Paul pleaded. "Just think for a while."

So we sat down while he thought. His thoughts were undoubtedly about how he was going to get rid of this preacher who insisted he find his family a house to rent, when he wasn't even involved in renting houses, but selling them. After a while though, he must have come to the conclusion that there was only one way to get rid of us—find us a house!

He finally snapped his fingers. "There is a man who moved to Arizona—he left an old farmhouse empty—I will call him!"

He telephoned Arizona. "Yes, I guess I could rent it. Charge the family sixty dollars a month." The realtor hadn't mentioned that we had five little children!

We drove out in the country, and waded through the winter's accumulation of snow. "Beautiful," we said. "We will move in next week."

And it was the most beautiful house we had ever seen. It is true that we were leaving a fancy ranch home near Toledo, Ohio. It is true that this house had sagging floors, no carpeting, peeled paint, three bedrooms upstairs and one small bathroom downstairs, but it was beautiful to us, because the Lord had provided it for us.

We left Hart to return to Toledo to get our children and possessions. We made it as far as Lansing, when our little Renault gave a final gasp and died. We sat there looking at each other. A man knocked on our car window. "Oh, excuse me! I have been following you. I thought you were one of my relatives who has a car just like yours. Since I am here, do you need some help?"

We surely did!

He helped us push the car off the road, took us to a gas station to arrange for them to tow the car there, and dropped us off at a bus station.

"We have a bus leaving for Toledo in just a few minutes," the clerk said. We boarded the Greyhound bus and Paul sat in the front seat so he could chat with the driver.

"Hey, ya'want a ride home?" the driver asked. "I'm running early tonight!"

Only God could arrange that the Greyhound bus dropped us off just half a block from our house!

We went to the man from whom we had been buying our ranch home. "Could you just forget our equity in the house, and take it back?" we asked him.

"I surely will!" he replied. "My son wants that house! He will really be happy with this news!"

The following week Paul deposited me, five weary children, and one large U-Haul trailer at our new home —at four o'clock in the morning. Then he went back to get the other U-Haul he had left at our home just across the border between Ohio and Michigan.

The kids and I slept on the floor, since the beds were packed firmly in the trailer. The next morning, I turned on the faucet to get water to start cleaning the house.

No water.

No water?

Paul arrived that afternoon, exhausted. "Hi," I greeted him. 'There is no water here!"

"No water?" the realtor exclaimed later. "I will send someone out to see what the problem is."

They found the problem. The well had run dry.

We met our new neighbors with pails in our hands. "May we borrow some water, please?" They generously shared their water with us for just over a month.

Paul called his uncle who was the minister of a small Wesleyan Methodist church nearby. "God has called me to the ministry. May I hold a revival meeting in your church?" he asked.

"The ministry!" his uncle exclaimed. "Don't go into the ministry, whatever you do!" For the next several minutes, Uncle Elmer tried to persuade Paul to do anything but become a preacher of the gospel. Months later, he told him, "I said those things to test you. If I could have talked you out of preaching, it would have been a sure sign that God had not called you. But if God had really called you, no man could talk you out of it."

Now he finally told Paul, "Okay, come to my church and hold a revival meeting."

I was terrified. Missions, junior church, ministering to people one at a time—that was not so frightening. But a revival meeting in a church was something else.

Just before the opening service was to begin, I was literally shaking. I knew God had called Paul to preach the gospel to the lost, and that didn't frighten me. But he was in a church tonight, preaching to the saved. I knew what God had told him to tell Christians—that many of them had never made a full commitment to Christ, were in a lukewarm, backslidden state, and they were not prepared to face persecution for Christ's sake.

I knew that most of the Christians of America would not appreciate being warned of coming persecution. A few weeks earlier, I had again questioned God as to the wisdom of Paul's preaching such an unpopular message. I had felt led to just pick up my Bible and open it and read the verses I found. I turned to a conversation between Jeremiah and God concerning Israel thousands of years before.

> *Then said I, Ah, Lord God! behold, the prophets say unto them, Ye shall not see the sword, neither shall ye have famine; but I will give you assured peace in this place.*
>
> *Then the Lord said unto me, The prophets prophesy lies in my name: I sent them not, neither have I commanded them, neither spake unto them: they prophesy unto you a false vision and divination, and a thing of nought, and the deceit of their heart.*
>
> *Therefore thus saith the Lord concerning the prophets that prophesy in my name, and I sent them not, yet they say, Sword and famine shall not be in this land; By sword and famine shall those prophets be consumed.*

*And the people to whom they prophesy shall
be cast out in the streets of Jerusalem because of
the famine and the sword.* (Jeremiah 14:13-16)

Then God led me in His Word to His call to Ezekiel,
and it helped me to better understand Paul's message.

*Son of man, speak to the children of thy peo-
ple, and say unto them, When I bring the sword
upon a land, if the people of the land take a man
of their coasts, and set him for their watchman:*

*If when he seeth the sword come upon the
land, he blow the trumpet, and warn the people;*

*Then whosoever heareth the sound of the
trumpet, and taketh not warning; if the sword
come, and take him away, his blood shall be
upon his own head.*

*He heard the sound of the trumpet, and took
not warning; his blood shall be upon him. But he
that taketh warning shall deliver his soul.*

*But if the watchman see the sword come, and
blow not the trumpet, and the people be not
warned; if the sword come, and take any person
from among them, he is taken away in his
iniquity; but his blood will I require at the
watchman's hand.* (Ezekiel 33:2-6)

I sincerely believed that God had called Paul to preach
the gospel to the lost and to be a watchman to warn the
church of troubled times ahead.

But now I felt like running from that little church.
Once again, I felt led to God's Word, and I picked up

44

my Bible, opened it at random, and read just one verse, *"For if the trumpet give an uncertain sound, who shall prepare himself to the battle?"* (I Corinthians 14:8).

The Word of God gave me strength along with the knowledge that God was with us, and that this was truly the message He had called Paul to preach to indifferent, lukewarm Christians.

I quit shaking and began praying, as faith drove fear from my heart. Paul preached the Word of God fearlessly, and many people were touched by God that week.

A preacher from a small church in the little town of Ferry, Michigan attended the meetings and booked us at his church. We just kept going from there, with God always giving us one or two more bookings at each meeting.

We had never been so happy in our lives. We loved serving God. We loved that old farmhouse—especially now that it had water! We loved each other and we loved our children. Nothing could mar our peace and joy and happiness. Serving the god of materialism had never brought the contentment God gave us when we began to serve Him.

Then Paul got deathly sick, and through his sickness, we learned more about this wonderful God we serve.

8

He maketh sore, and bindeth up: he woundeth, and his hands make whole. (Job 5:18)

Paul had pneumonia. I had never seen him so sick, as he lay in bed with a raging fever.

We had no employer but God, no income but what He provided. He had used churches to provide for us, but now Paul was unable to preach, so our income had come to a sudden stop.

I went to the kitchen one morning. "Lord," I prayed, "do you see how much food I have left? There is only enough for one more meal. You told us in your Word not to worry about food, but how can I help but worry when I am out if it? We have put you first. God, we need your help—today!"

By the time I had finished praying, I was crying with frustration. Could I trust God enough to believe He would provide food for an insignificant family living in a tiny pinprick of the earth which is just a small part of the vast universe He controls?

I waged a battle of faith and fear that day. One moment I sincerely believed God cared enough to send us food; the next minute I thought I was crazy to even expect Him to.

I fed our children at noon. That was it. There was simply no more food in our house. There was no money to buy any. I had decided I was not going to ask anyone but God for help. He was our employer. People hadn't called Paul to leave his job and preach the gospel! The United States government shouldn't have to help us. We were God's responsibility!

After lunch, the telephone rang. An elderly couple from Scottville, about forty miles from our home, asked if we would stay home. "We are coming to visit you this afternoon."

"Great," I groaned, hanging up the telephone. "Just what I need. Company. No food. Paul sick. I'm here trying to pray. And a couple I met once several weeks before and just vaguely remember, are coming to visit us."

A couple of hours later, I saw them drive up in a station wagon. I tried to smile and greet them enthusiastically.

"Come here," they said, leading me to their car. "We brought something to you."

I looked in the car. The seats had been laid flat, and their station wagon was literally stuffed full of food. I was astounded.

"Why—why did you bring all this?"

They answered, "The Lord told us you had a need. We couldn't get you people off our minds, and we felt we had to bring you food. So we gathered some out of our cupboards and then went to some of our Christian relatives and told them what the Lord had impressed us to do. They gave us food to bring you too. And here it is."

We spent nearly an hour transferring the food from their car to our cupboards and refrigerator. I was in a

47

daze. There were fifty pounds of sugar, real dairy butter, dozens of eggs, fresh vegetables and fruits, and more meat than we could eat in a month. My refrigerator and cupboards were filled and the kitchen counter tops and floor were still full of food.

Even when I had spurts of faith while asking God for food earlier that afternoon, I surely hadn't expected Him to answer by filling my house with it!

Paul's fever broke, and he began to recover that very day.

God had put us in a position where we could only look to Him for help. And He had proven He was a faithful employer, with sick leave benefits, whom we could depend upon to provide for all of our needs.

9

Verily I say unto you, There is no man that hath left house, or brethren, or sisters, or father, or mother, or wife, or children, or lands, for my sake, and the gospel's, But he shall receive an hundredfold now in this time, houses, and brethren, and sisters, and mothers, and children, and lands, with persecutions,—and in the world to come eternal life. (Mark 10.29-30)

We lived peacefully in that country home for six happy months, while serving the Lord in any church that would invite us to hold a revival meeting. Then the realtor called us. "The owner of the house you are living in has decided to sell it. We will give you an opportunity to purchase it for $8,500. We only require a $1,500 down payment."

He may as well have said $15 million for a down payment!

"If you can't buy it, plan on being out in thirty days— that will be October 1."

October 1—a familiar date. Our sixth baby was due on that date and we had a revival meeting booked on that date. Now we added to our calendar, "Move."

But where? We discovered that landlords are not too enthusiastic about renting to a family of seven, and we really didn't blame them.

We frantically ran down every lead we could get. We drove on country roads, looking for an empty house. When we would find one that looked habitable, we would go to the house next to it and ask if they could tell us how to contact the owner. All of this led to nothing.

Finally, September was nearly over, and we had no house to move into. Paul drove through the town of Shelby, six miles south of Hart. A "For Sale" sign, tacked to a tree in front of a huge white house with pillars and a beautiful front porch caught his eye.

That is your house, he heard the Lord impress upon his mind.

"But, Lord," he argued, "it is for sale, not for rent. We can't buy a house with no money!"

The next day Paul found himself driving past the house again. That little "For Sale" sign drew his eyes like a magnet. He pulled into the driveway.

This is your house, the Lord spoke again.

"It's too nice—too big! We can't even buy the one we are living in now for $8,500!" And he backed out again.

We had a few days left before the fateful October 1. Paul continued searching, but that big white house kept appearing in his mind, and God continued to urge him to contact the owners. Twice now he had driven in and out of the driveway.

Now he drove in again, turned off the car engine, and just sat and looked at the house. This was foolish! How could a poor preacher, whose only employer was the Lord, who didn't receive a salary, who was living totally by faith, who had no money for a down payment, call someone about buying a house?

Finally, he gave in. He called the telephone number penciled beneath the "For Sale" sign.

"Hi," he said. "I am a preacher—a poor one. I don't have any money, but I am interested in buying your house on a land contract, with no money down."

"There, Lord," Paul said silently. "I have done what I felt you wanted me to do."

Instead of the crash of the receiver Paul expected to hear, a kind voice replied, "Fine. We will meet you tomorrow at the house and show it to you!"

We were there!

"Our father died, and we inherited this house from him," the brother and sister who met us said. "We will sell it to you on a land contract with no money down. We are asking $15,000 for the house."

Even if we could buy it, how could we possibly pay the monthly payments? It was hard enough to pay our sixty dollars monthly rent! But since we were here, we looked at it. It was beautiful. We went through the large living room, dining room, a huge office with a separate entrance, two bathrooms, three bedrooms, a laundry room, a nice kitchen—and this was just the downstairs! We looked toward the beautiful open stairway leading from the front entrance.

"I don't know if we can see that today," the owners said. "It is a separate apartment, and it is rented. We rent it for $105 a month."

One hundred five dollars a month? Then we *could* make the payments!

"Why don't we meet here again tomorrow," the owners suggested. "We will get some figures from the bank and you write down what you can do, and we will see if we can get together."

Paul decided that evening to try to put the payments at about $150 a month. The next morning, he called the local bank. "We would like to pay payments of about $150 a month on a $15,000 house," he told the person from the mortgage department. "Could you tell us how many years it would take? We haven't discussed interest, but just figure 7 percent for now."

"One hundred fifty-four dollars and twenty-six cents a month. Twelve years," was the clipped reply.

We pulled out a little piece of paper at our meeting the next day, and handed it to one of the owners.

"Look," he exclaimed, producing his figures. I have the very same figures! I decided on 7 percent interest and a twelve-year mortgage too! If you want to, we can have the deal closed this week!"

All the time we had been frantically scouring the area for a house to rent, God had an empty house waiting for us to buy, with no down payment, and an upstairs apartment providing the major portion of the monthly payments!

On October 1, we moved into our new house. And by the time our new sweet baby, Debbie, came three weeks later, we were all settled and impatiently awaiting her arrival.

Each experience in our faith walk was teaching us to trust God completely to take care of us, and not to underestimate His power to soften and prepare the hearts of men.

10

Repent ye therefore, and be converted, that your sins may be blotted out, when the times of refreshing shall come from the presence of the Lord. (Acts 3:19)

Many pastors throughout Michigan opened their church doors to us. We were not booked more than two or three meetings ahead, but God always provided a place for Paul to minister. God blessed the meetings with many people being saved and Christians being revived.

Sunday school teachers, deacons and youth leaders were among those saved. Pastors and their wives were among those who found again their first love for Jesus Christ. Altars were usually filled with people weeping their way to Christ.

During one meeting in Grant, Michigan, Paul gave an invitation to come to the altar for salvation and the filling of the Holy Ghost, and the entire congregation knelt, weeping. Paul looked on, amazed at what the Lord was doing. At nine-thirty that evening, he sat down behind the pulpit. The service continued until eleven o'clock, led by God alone. Grudges long nourished were confessed and forgiven. Husbands and wives found their first love again, and rebellious young people asked their parents for forgiveness and hugged them for the first time in years. The love of God swept over that congregation and drove out the bitterness that had accumulated over the years. One little boy stood up, and between sobs, told the congregation that Jesus had cleaned out his heart, swept away the cobwebs, and scrubbed all the dirt away with His blood. "Jesus is a good janitor!" he concluded.

An elderly lady stood up and told the people, "Friends, I have spent most of my life as a registered nurse. I have been with countless people at their deaths. Years ago, many people turned to God on their deathbeds, crying out to Jesus Christ to become their Savior. But today, it is no longer that way. We seldom see a deathbed repentance. Doctors have their patients drugged to escape pain, and their minds are not often even capable of receiving Christ into their hearts. They are slipping into eternity without God to spend thousands of years in pain, in hell."

"Friends, if you intend to receive Jesus as your Savior, do it *now*, while you are still able to make a decision. Don't expect to make peace with God when you are dying. You probably will never have that chance, and it will be forever too late for you."

"Folks, if you plan to lead your loved ones to Jesus Christ, do it now, while they can still comprehend what you are saying. The Bible says, *'Now is the accepted time; behold, now is the day of salvation'* " (II Corinthians 6:2).

There was a hush when she sat down, as the Holy Spirit drove her words into the hearts of those people.

The congregation spent four hours in church that evening, and no one wanted to go home. When God moves by His Spirit and among His people, church is exciting for even the children. Too often, church services are merely a form of worship, rather than true worship by the people for their God; songs are sung without feeling, rather than Christians making a joyful noise unto God in true praise and thanksgiving; a sermon is delivered as a lecture, rather than as an anointed message from God to His people, through a pastor who is only a dedicated vessel for God to speak through.

Paul had rebelled against preaching, but there was no doubt he was called by God to preach, because God was blessing his unpolished sermons with results that only God can produce: salvation, the filling of the Holy Ghost, restoring the joy of salvation to depressed people, the mending of broken spirits, and the flow of love restored among God's people.

God was also healing the sick. Every Sunday evening, the final service of the revival meetings, Paul would ask the sick to come for prayer. They came! Every healing service, no matter what town we were in or what size the church, would be packed. God healed people with deaf ears, cancer, leukemia, tumors, back trouble, cerebral palsy—all forms of sicknesses.

Before every healing service, Paul told me he felt as if he were walking by faith out on a tree limb, praying it wouldn't break. But then the anointing of the Holy Spirit would come upon him, and all doubts would leave, and God would touch the people with His healing power.

One day we were invited to a little community church in a town a few miles from our home. Paul was to preach until the congregation found a new pastor.

Paul's first message in that church was on Christmas Sunday. "Born to Die" was his message, and nearly half the congregation, including many leaders of the church, came forward during the altar call to be saved.

People who had attended church faithfully for years realized that to them Jesus Christ was merely a historical figure, not a personal Savior and Lord.

Their salvation made an impact on the entire community. One young man, who owned a carry-out store, threw out all his liquor, filthy magazines and cigarettes. Today, he has a Christian bookstore there.

Another man returned items he had carried out of the large factory he worked in, confessing to the manager that he had stolen them. He also paid the factory hundreds of dollars for other things he had taken.

A fireman, whom we led to the Lord in his home shortly after the meeting, began for the first time since he began hunting, to obey the one-deer limit allowed to Michigan residents—and he did that during hunting season!

Those new Christians were so hungry to hear the Word of God, that some of them would be at our home every day, asking to be taught more of the truths of God's Word. After about three weeks of teaching day and night, Paul invited them to come all at once on Monday evenings to study the Word together.

They filled our living room, dining room and office! We had some beautiful meetings, singing praises to God, studying the Scriptures and praying together.

Then one Monday morning, we woke up to a cold house. We looked at each other, and both of us said in unison, "Oh, no."

We knew what had happened. We were behind with our gas bill, and the gas company had disconnected our gas supply. And it was winter in Michigan!

Why had God allowed us to get in this predicament, we wondered. It seemed to us a terrible testimony for a preacher to have his gas turned off!

Finally we were able to pray, "Lord, this is your problem. We are your problem. You said you would take care of us, if we sought you first. So you are the only one we are going to tell about this. Please give us the money to pay our bill and get our gas back on."

Monday afternoon—the house was getting colder by the minute, and we had a meeting that night! What would new Christians think about us having our gas turned off? Would it damage their childlike faith in God?

Paul went to a friend of his, who owned a roller skating arena. "Nick," he asked, "could I borrow some of your electric heaters tonight?"

"Sure," Nick replied, and thankfully did not question Paul further.

Paul came home and placed the electric heaters behind our furniture, out of sight. We closed off the rest of the house, and when our new friends arrived that evening, the house was warm, and we had a beautiful service.

After everyone had left, we piled blankets and quilts on the kids, and snuggled down under a mass of blankets ourselves. In the morning, it was colder. About 8:45 a.m., there was a knock at our door. An elderly Christian gentleman stood there. He had driven from a city about forty miles south of us.

"Brother Wilde, I have to talk to you," he said. Paul could see that he was troubled, and invited him in to sit down.

"No, no, I can't stay. I just need some help. I don't even know how to say this, because I don't understand it myself. But early this morning, I got down on my knees to pray. I couldn't pray. I would start to pray, and I would hear the word '*gas.*' This happened several times. I finally said, 'Lord, is this you? If it is, what do you mean?' And the Lord spoke to my heart and said, '*You go ask Paul Wilde what I mean. He will tell you.*' So I have driven here this morning to find out if you know what all this means."

"I surely do!" Paul answered. "My gas was turned off yesterday, because we are behind with our bill!"

"Oh! Is that it? Good! How much is it? I will pay it right away!"

Paul hated to tell him the amount. "Almost $300," he said hesitantly.

"Great! I will go to a local bank and get a money order made out to the gas company, and you can call them and tell them the money is on the way. Praise the Lord! I feel better! I couldn't understand what this was all about!"

He wasn't the only one who felt better! We rejoiced in the Lord for sending one of His servants to pay our gas bill. We don't understand why God waited until the gas was shut off to send the money. But we do know, after living by faith for ten years, that God always waits until the last possible second to send the answer. His Word says, *"The trying of your faith worketh patience.*

But let patience have her perfect work, that ye may be perfect and entire, wanting nothing" (James 1:3-4).

We also know that if we put our trust in God—not in people, not in our government, but in God alone—that He takes care of us beautifully and bountifully.

What a great God we serve! What a loving Father we have! And what a wonderful Employer!

11

I have been young, and now am old; yet have I not seen the righteous forsaken, nor his seed begging bread. (Psalm 37:25)

One Monday evening, five of the men who came regularly to our home meetings came to our home a few minutes before the service was to start. They asked to talk to Paul privately in his office.

"We have decided to pay you a salary," they said. "You just give us a weekly report of what you have done during the week, and how many souls you have won to the Lord, and we will provide for the needs of you and your family."

"What did you tell them?" I asked him, as he told me about it later.

"I told them I am working for the Lord, and report only to Him and am supported only by Him. They meant well, but didn't understand that my whole life has already been given to God, and I can't take it back and give it to men."

"Were they upset?" I asked.

"I think so—yes."

They were upset. They had been giving us money and food, but their gifts stopped coming after that evening.

We learned we had become dependent upon their support, instead of looking to God alone. Since that time, we have found that every single time we began to depend on people who were faithfully supporting us, God would see that their support would be withdrawn from us, so we would depend on Him alone. If someone would tell us they would buy something for our church or office, it would be easy to just depend on them for that particular thing, instead of looking to God as our source. We have learned time and time again that men cannot be depended upon—only God can.

The Bible says, *"Cursed be the man that trusteth in man, and maketh flesh his arm, and whose heart departeth from the Lord"* (Jeremiah 17:5).

Now we were left looking to God alone again, seemingly forsaken by men. It was Saturday, the day before Easter. Again, my cupboards were nearly empty. I had only enough to feed my six children the rest of the day. There would be no Easter dinner unless the Lord provided the food!

About six-thirty that evening our next-door neighbors knocked at our door. Phyllis handed me a huge roast. She said, "I feel sort of funny bringing this. Will you take it? I just felt like I should bring it over for your dinner tomorrow."

My eyes filled with tears as I took the roast from her. "Thank you," I said. "Thank you, Lord," I whispered as I put it in my refrigerator. "Bless our neighbors abundantly for their help."

Phyllis's husband, Bob, handed Paul a box. "It isn't much, just some pennies I have saved over the years. I thought I should bring them to you."

Just some pennies! A box fall of pennies that day, when our need was so great, was a priceless gift from our wonderful God, given through one of His vessels.

Phyllis and Bob were members of a Bible Baptist church. They had never given us food or money before, and have never given us anything since that day. God proved to us through them that our faith should be in Him alone; that even when we cannot see how God can provide for us, and it seems that our Christian friends have all forsaken us, God will still find a way to provide for the needs of His children.

A few days later, our cupboards were again nearly empty. I was feeding Debbie, and Paul was helping me with the other children, by fixing their breakfast. He opened the refrigerator. There were some eggs left.

"Okay, Lord, I will fix eggs for the children today. But while I am frying the eggs, will you please send us some bread, so they can have toast with them?" The eggs were cooked, and the children gathered around the table to eat. They had just thanked the Lord for their eggs, when someone knocked at our kitchen door. Paul opened the door. An elderly gentleman from a town about eight miles away stood at our door. He had a paper sack in his hand.

"Brother Wilde, my wife insisted I bring this to you right now."

"What is it?" Paul asked.

"Well, she baked bread this morning. This loaf fell, and doesn't look so good, but she told me to bring it to you anyway. I told her she should wait until the other loaf was done, because it would probably look better, but she insisted on my coming right away with this loaf."

Paul opened the sack. There was the most beautiful loaf of bread we had ever laid eyes upon. A million dollars would not have been as appreciated as that loaf of bread Paul had prayed for, and God had sent.

The gentleman shook Paul's hand, leaving a five-dollar bill in it, and left.

We cried and thanked God for the bread and the money. Just then we heard another knock at our door. The same gentleman stood there weeping uncontrollably.

"What is the matter?" Paul asked. "Were you in an accident? What is wrong?"

"The Lord told me to give you ten dollars," he answered sobbing, "and I only gave you five! Here is the other five." And he left again.

What a time we had around our table that morning, praising God and thanking Him for the bread, the woman who had baked it, and the man who had delivered it!

Kathy came to me one day and said, "Mommy, I need new shoes. These hurt my feet."

We didn't have the money that day to buy her a pair of shoes, so I said, "Kathy, why don't you pray and ask God to bring you some shoes?"

She went into her room and got on her knees by her bed, and asked God for shoes. Within seven days, Kathy had five pairs of beautiful shoes that fit her perfectly. One pair was sent by Paul's aunt from California!

Jesus told Philip two thousand years earlier, "Whatsoever ye shall ask in my name, that will I do, that the Father may be glorified in the Son" (John 14:13).

What a promise! The best part of it is that it stills works for God's children *today*. God is *real*, and He cares about every single person He has created. He has the hairs of our heads numbered. We don't even know how many hairs we have on our heads!

Many times, we Christians in America do not experience God providing miraculously for us, because we provide so abundantly for ourselves. We provide for our own needs and our desires first—and then give our leftovers to God's work and to those who have needs. We give to God only out of our abundance, fearing to give as the widow whom Jesus commended gave. She gave *all her living*. Do you believe that after that sacrificial gift, God let her starve to death? I believe He provided abundantly for her!

We Americans give to God out of our abundance, rather than sacrificially. We are afraid to trust God as a child trusts his parents to provide for us. We are afraid to allow ourselves to get in a position, wherein God either provides for us or we go without!

Paul and I and our eight children have been in that position many, many times, and God has always fed us, clothed us, and provided shelter for us, above what we could ask or think. We have never once been without a meal. If God can provide for our family of ten, He can provide for anyone who will simply put Him first in his life and place his hand securely in His and trust Him completely as his source. Jesus said, *"If ye then being evil, know how to give good gifts unto your children, how much more shall your Father which is in heaven give good things to them that ask him?"* (Matthew 7:11).

If we Christians in America look to ourselves as our own source, will we panic when famine comes to our country? Man is helpless during famine. But if our trust and faith are in God rather than ourselves, we have His promise, *"The eye of the Lord is upon them that fear him, upon them that hope in his mercy; to deliver their soul from death, and to keep them alive in famine"* (Psalm 33:18-19).

Would we be able to trust in our own capabilities if war were to come to our country? David said, *"Our soul waiteth for the Lord: he is our help and our shield. For our heart shall rejoice in him, because we have trusted in his holy name"* (Psalm 33:20-21).

Most of God's children know the end time is fast approaching. But we need not fear, if our trust is in God, rather than in ourselves, our jobs, our paychecks. The Bible says, *"The Lord knoweth the days of the upright: and their inheritance shall be for ever. They shall not be ashamed in the evil time: and in the days of famine they shall be satisfied"* (Psalm 37:18-19).

Time and time again, God proved to us, as we put His Word to the test, that He is a God we can depend on and His Word will not fail.

One day, I had quite a few groceries in my house, but I needed eggs.

"Am I greedy to ask for eggs?" I wondered. I don't have to have them. We can surely live without them!"

I decided to ask anyway. "God, I would like you to send me some eggs, please," I prayed simply.

The telephone rang later that afternoon. A man from a town about twelve miles from us asked if we would come to his home and visit with him and his wife.

We went, and as we were leaving his house, he handed me three dozen eggs. Nothing else—just eggs. It strengthened my faith far more than if he had given me a box of groceries with eggs in it!

The next morning when we opened our back door, there were three dozen eggs on our step! We learned later that the man we had visited the night before had brought us another three dozen eggs early in the morning when we were still asleep. I had asked our Father for eggs—and less than a day later, He had given us six dozen!

We were to discover that we could trust God to provide not only bread, a dinner, eggs, and shoes, but also cars!

12

My God shall supply all your need according to his riches in glory by Christ Jesus. (Philippians 4:19)

O ur station wagon was wearing out fast, taking us from church to church in towns and cities all over Michigan. In fact it was using nearly as much oil as it was gasoline!

Paul was concerned about it getting us to out next meeting. The day we were to leave for Luther, Michigan, to hold services in a Pilgrim Holiness church, Paul went into our garage. He shut the door behind him and pulled the curtains closed, covering the windows. He didn't want the neighbors to see what he was about to do.

Then he laid hands on the car and began to pray. "Father, you said to lay hands on the sick and they would recover. I know this works for people, and I hope it works for this car. Please heal this car and help it make one more meeting, Lord, in Jesus' name."

The car got us to Luther. Paul preached from his heart there, and most of the people responded to the Word of God. But there was one man who was there every service and never responded in any way to the messages. "He either doesn't like me or he doesn't like what I am preaching," Paul said to me after one service.

At the close of the meetings, nearly everyone had been revived except this one man. Paul had finished loading our station wagon, and was standing by the church talking to the preacher, when he felt someone tap him on the shoulder. It was a dark night, and he thought he and the preacher were alone. He whirled around and faced the man who had sat motionless during all the services.

"Come here," the man said, and Paul followed him to the front of the church. He thought for sure he was going to find out if he had enough of God's love to turn the other cheek when he was hit!

"The Lord told me," the man said slowly, "to give you a car."

"What?" Paul shouted. "He *what*?"

"He told me to give you a car. That one," he said, pointing to a two-year-old Chevrolet Impala. His wife and children were sitting in it. "I fix up cars that have been damaged, and sell them. I owe some back tithes to the Lord. The car has thirty-thousand miles on it. You wait right here. I will be back with the title."

Paul was in a daze as he returned to the pastor of the church. "What did he want?" the pastor asked.

"He gave me his car," Paul answered hesitantly, glancing at the pastor's old car.

"He what?" the pastor shouted.

"He gave me his car!"

A few minutes later, the man returned to the church. He had somewhere found a notary public at eleven o'clock on a Sunday night. He handed Paul the title with a twenty-dollar bill wrapped in it. "The twenty

dollars is for you to get the car's new tires balanced."
And he left.

We returned home in our new car, praising and
thanking God for His gift. We hadn't had enough faith
to ask God to give us a car, but He gave us one anyway.

We continued to travel to large churches and small
churches. We took the offerings they gave us, no matter
how small or large they were, and praised God for
them. Sometimes the offerings were generous. Other
times they were not nearly enough to even cover our expenses.

We spent five days in one church in Traverse City,
Michigan, and were given thirty-seven dollars at the
close of the meetings. That was in 1970. We had six
children to support, and had paid our own traveling expenses. But God never failed us. We just thanked God
for the thirty-seven dollars, and trusted Him, not churches, to take care of us.

One day we asked Him to send us money so we could
pay some bills. As usual, we couldn't even imagine
where the money would come from, but just trusted
God to find a way to send us some. After all, we knew
that "faith is the evidence of things not seen" (Hebrews
11:1). That afternoon, there was a loud, insistent knock
at our door. Paul went to the door and found an irate
young man standing there.

He shouted, "I have had it! My car just quit out in
front of your house. I hate that car! I kicked it, and hurt
my foot. Here! Here are the keys. I don't want it. I
don't ever want to see it again. It's all yours. Just let me
use your telephone, and I will get out of here and leave

the car to you. It's yours, Mister. The title is in the glove box."

He telephoned his brother to come and get him and left.

Paul went out to look at his newly acquired car. "Not bad," he thought, as he looked it over. He opened the hood, reached in and uncrossed two wires. He got in the car, started it up, and it ran beautifully.

Thirty minutes after an angry young man had stood in front of our house, kicking his car because it wouldn't run, we had a nice car, that ran beautifully, parked in front of our house with a "For Sale" sign on it. We sold it that week and paid our bills.

Another time when we needed money, Paul came home and said, "I can't understand it, but I feel I am supposed to buy a car I saw today. It is nearly new, We can't afford it, but I think God wants us to buy it."

"But we already have a car," I argued. "The one that man gave us in Luther still runs beautifully. We don't need another car."

"I know it. Maybe God knows something is wrong with our car—something I don't know about. All I know is that I feel God wants us to buy this car."

"Okay, we will buy it then." But inside I couldn't believe God would lead us to get in debt by purchasing a newer car, when we had a perfectly good one we didn't owe anything on. Paul financed the car through the bank, and parked his other car in our front yard to sell. Almost immediately, a gentleman stopped to look at it.

"I don't know. It's not really what I want. I want one a little newer." He stayed and kept looking it over.

"What are you going to buy when you sell this?" he finally asked.

"I already bought one. It's in my garage," Paul answered. "Do you want to see it?"

Paul took him to the garage.

"This is just exactly what I am looking for!" the man said excitedly. "Sell this one to me! How much can I buy it for?"

Paul named a figure $600 above what he had just paid for the car.

"Sold!" the man said, and wrote him a check. He left with our new car, leaving us with our old car still parked in the front yard with a "For Sale" sign on it, and $600 to pay our bills with!

Our faith in God began as a tiny mustard seed, but as we learned that God readily supplied all our needs as we spent our lives laboring in His harvest field, our faith in Him was growing daily. And we would need greater faith, because God was about to lead us into trusting Him not only for the needs of our family, but for the needs of an expanding ministry.

13

I will sing unto the Lord as long as I live: I will sing praise to my God while I have my being. (Psalm 104:33)

Delight thyself also in the Lord; and he shall give thee the desires of thine heart. (Psalm 37:4)

Paul and I loved to sing together. He enjoyed playing his saxophone and I enjoyed accompanying him on the piano or organ. A desire of his heart was to cut a recording of our own. One day he decided to do it, even though we did not have the money to pay a recording studio. He called Heart Warming Record Company, and managed to persuade them to let us audition for them. If they thought our records would sell, they would pay to have us recorded. They didn't give Paul much hope though, because we were unknown to both them and the public.

Paul took our car down to the car wash, put a quarter in the slot, and began washing his car. He heard God say, *Call Jimmy Swaggart. Tell him you want to cut a record.*

"Jimmy Swaggart?" Paul thought. "Why would he be interested? He doesn't even know me."

God did not give him any explanation or further advice.

When Paul came home, he said, "Carolyn, the Lord told me to call Jimmy Swaggart."

"Jimmy Swaggart? What on earth for?"

"I don't know. God just said to tell him I want to cut a record."

"What? Why would he be interested? He doesn't know you."

Paul went to our pile of Christian albums. "Here is one by Jimmy Swaggart. It says on the back that he lives in Baton Rouge, Louisiana."

Paul dialed information and got his number. "I would like to speak to Jimmy Swaggart, please," he said.

"He is in Flint, Michigan," came the southern drawl. Flint, Michigan! Flint was only about an hour's drive from our home—quite a bit closer than Baton Rouge, Louisiana!

Paul asked what motel he was in and called there. "Brother Swaggart," he began, "you don't know me. I am a preacher from Michigan. The Lord told me to call you and tell you I want to cut a record album of our music."

"I have been thinking about helping some preacher get started with records," he replied. "I'll tell you what, chief. You send me a tape of your music, and I will see what I can do."

"Could I bring a tape to you while you are in Flint?" Paul questioned.

"That will be okay. How about tomorrow afternoon?"

Needless to say, we spent the rest of that day and half of the night trying to come up with a perfect tape of our music. The next day we were playing it for Jimmy Swaggart in a Flint motel.

"Shut it off, shut it off," he said after about two songs had been played. "You should have five records. The way to make the most profit from them is to do it yourself. I have my front covers made in Japan, the back covers in...."

"I can't afford to do it myself," Paul interrupted.

"Okay. I will sponsor your first album then. You leave me your telephone number and go back home. I will be in touch with you in a few days."

Paul picked up his tape recorder, thanked Brother Swaggart for his time, and we went back home. About a week passed. We figured Jimmy Swaggart had more important things on his mind than us, and we didn't really expect to hear from him.

Then he called, "Hi, chief, how are you doing? I've got you set up to go to Oklahoma City and cut your record there. You will have to get a color transparency for your front cover, and pay your traveling expenses. What instruments do you want to back you up?"

About three weeks later, we were in Oklahoma City, cutting a record, completely paid for by Jimmy Swaggart. It was a singing album with one saxophone number on it.

A month later, Jimmy Swaggart called us again. "Hey, doc, I just heard your record! Why didn't you tell me you played the saxophone?"

"I had some sax numbers on the tape," Paul explained, "but you told me to shut it off before I got to them."

"Well, you get right back to Oklahoma City and cut a saxophone record. The sax is one of my favorite instruments. I will pay for it. What do you want for background? Violins? Voices?"

"Voices," Paul quickly answered, wanting the people to hear the words as well as the tunes of the songs.

A few weeks later, we were back in Oklahoma City, recording a second album, paid for by Jimmy Swaggart. When the saxophone album was released, he played it on his radio program for a week, and sold over twenty-five hundred albums.

Those two albums were a tremendous help to us. All the while we were traveling in evangelistic work, the profits we received from the sale of the records completely covered our travel expenses. And we know they have blessed others too. Just a few months ago, eight years after the records were cut, a man called us and said he was preparing to commit suicide, but was gloriously saved by turning to Jesus while listening to the song, *He Touched Me* on our first album.

We stayed at a motel in Oklahoma, and in a dream that night Paul saw a bus he was to purchase. He told me about it in the morning, and I promptly forgot about it. Later that day as we passed through Missouri, Paul squealed to a stop. "What happened?" I cried.

"I just saw the bus I dreamed about last night. It's up on a hill. We just passed it!" We turned around and went back to the bus. "How much is it?" Paul asked.

"Three-thousand, three hundred dollars," was the reply.

"I will be back to get it next week," Paul told him.

The following week he got the bus and returned home with it in a raging blizzard. We financed it, knowing that the bus payments would be less than motel expenses. After using the bus for a year, we sold it for $4,700.

We traveled all over Michigan, holding revival meetings in churches during the weekends. We also continued having home meetings. We had so many people coming that our house couldn't hold them. We were wondering what to do about the problem when Paul went downstairs and looked at the old stone basement. He came bounding upstairs. "We will fix it up!" he said. "It should hold about eighty people!"

"The basement? It's filthy! It's awful!"

"It will be beautiful. I will spray all the stones white to brighten it up a bit."

A few weeks later, it was beautiful. It was painted white, the floor was freshly painted, Paul had built a nice altar rail at the front, and it was even equipped with a nice organ. We had some beautiful services in that old basement. People came from all over Michigan and surrounding states to fellowship with us. The sick were healed, souls were saved, and the captives were set free in our basement church. We always had a good time making a joyful noise unto the Lord, with people playing guitars, a banjo, saxophones, and an organ.

I was expecting our seventh child. We had four girls and two boys, and were anxiously awaiting the arrival of Stephen. I went to the doctor with a speech all prepared for him. "I was in the hospital five minutes before my first child arrived. I was in the hospital two minutes before the last one arrived. You doctors never arrive in time, so will you give me a discount if a nurse delivers him?" I asked.

"No. Full price, whether I am here or not!" he answered.

"What am I paying you for, if you are not even here when he comes?" I asked him.

"You are paying me in case something goes wrong," he answered.

"I can trust the Lord for that," I thought as I left his office. "I wonder if Paul will be my 'midwife'."

Our seventh child was brought safely into this world by Paul. It took us a few days though to abandon the name Stephen for Elizabeth!

Shortly after our beautiful little Elizabeth arrived, we made a big mistake in our faith walk.

14

Trust in the Lord with all thine heart; and lean not unto thine own understanding. In all thy ways acknowledge him, and he shall direct thy paths. (Proverbs 3:5-6)
In thee, O Lord, do I put my trust: let me never be put to confusion. (Psalm 71:1)

Paul knew God was leading him to start a church in Muskegon, Michigan. He contacted the owner of a nice, empty brick church in an excellent location. The owner told him he would lease it to him for $500 a month, but then changed his mind and agreed to rent it to him for $125 a month. We believed God had softened the man's heart, and we could hardly wait to share our good news with the people who were coming to our home meetings.

"We are not driving to Muskegon!" they said. One brother said, I don't believe the Lord is leading you in this at all. There is already a fine church in Muskegon and it would be similar to one you would start. Why not just work with the pastor, instead of you both going separate ways?"

We went to meet the pastor. He welcomed us enthusiastically. Paul held meetings in his church and many souls were saved. The pastor called his parent church in Detroit, a church of about five-thousand members, and arranged to have Paul speak there. After

Paul had preached there, they decided that Paul would become an evangelist in their churches.

The day we were to join the organization, the Lord stopped us. *No*, He said, *This is not the way I want you to go.*

We had not joined a denomination since being in the ministry. We just went to any church we were invited to, and preached the gospel of Jesus Christ.

Paul had been preaching in many Wesleyan churches, and was introduced at the annual Wesleyan camp meeting to all the Wesleyan pastors, but although we thought it was a fine denomination and enjoyed working in its churches, we had not become members. When it later became a requirement for evangelists to join the denomination to continue working in the Wesleyan churches, Paul quit preaching in them, rather than join.

Now again God was saying no to becoming part of a church and working exclusively in it. Our brothers and sisters in Christ who were part of the church did not understand our refusal to join it, and some said we were withdrawing ourselves from the body of Christ. But the body of Christ is bigger than any church or denomination that wraps itself in its pet doctrines, and excludes all others from the family of God.

We were now parted from the church in Muskegon that was supposed to be the reason we should not obey God and start a church in Muskegon. The people who attended our home meetings continued to say, "We will not go with you to Muskegon. If you go, you will go alone." They were wrong. If we had gone, we would have gone with God!

We were confused. The advice and counsel of man had brought confusion to the commandment of God. We have learned since that day never to consult men when we know what God is leading us to do. We have learned that men will invariably try to talk us out of doing what God has told us to do! We have also learned to obey God, even if everyone else thinks we are wrong. (And they usually do!) The opinions of men cannot be weighed against the commandments of God. God says that *"the foolishness of God is wiser than men"* (I Corinthians 1:25).

Moses, Daniel, Elijah and David went to the mountain, prayed, rebuked the king, and slew the giant, by themselves, following God alone. Jesus went to the cross alone, after rebuking Peter and addressing him as Satan, when he had advised Jesus against dying.

Many times when God speaks to men, Satan will use the advice of men to bring utter confusion and bewilderment to God's clear direction. God would have to lead us in other directions for three years before we had learned this crucial lesson in our faith walk, and before He could effectively use us in Muskegon, the post He had called us to.

While we had been in Oklahoma taping our record, we had visited a friend of ours in Dallas, Texas, Mr. Hollis. He had taken us to meet Gordon Lindsay. Although Gordon Lindsay had founded a great and successful ministry, *Christ for the Nations*, he was a humble servant of God.

Now Mr. Hollis telephoned us from Texas and invited us to sing at the International Convention of the

Full Gospel Fellowship of Churches and Ministers International. He said that Gordon Lindsay had agreed to introduce us to the gathering of thousands of preachers, and tell them we were available for evangelistic meetings in their churches. We were thrilled that God had given us this tremendous opportunity and we praised Him for it.

The Sunday before we were to leave for Tulsa, where the convention was to be held, Paul had been invited by Lester Sumrall to speak at his church in South Bend, Indiana. We were excited about our coming trip. It was our big break! Then God spoke in the still, small voice He uses to guide His people. We could go to South Bend, but we were not to go on to Tulsa!

Paul was really disappointed. "Why, God?" he questioned. "This is our big opportunity! I will be booked way ahead, instead of the one or two meetings you have been giving me ahead."

God didn't bother to explain what His reasons were. He seldom does. This is part of the faith walk. The city we are walking towards is the New Jerusalem, and God usually shows us where to walk only one step at a time, and we are not always sure why that step leads in the direction it does!

Paul had been so sure this opportunity was from the Lord. "Probably it is the voice of the devil that is telling me not to go," he decided. "I will go anyway."

Two days before we were to leave for South Bend and Tulsa, I was troubled all day. I felt that either we would be in an accident if we went or one of our children would be hurt while we were gone.

I didn't tell Paul my feelings. I felt that whether or not we went was between him and God. My responsibility was to submit to Paul's decision, right or wrong. But I was afraid to go and my mind was in turmoil.

About six o'clock that evening some friends called us. "We have sold some things at a flea market today," they said. "We would like to give you the money for your trip. Could you come and get it?"

Paul left for their town, six miles away. On his way back home, his mind was still in turmoil about whether or not he should go. "God, show me what to do," he prayed. "I want to know for sure what your will is." Then he saw a truck passing a line of cars, heading straight for him. Paul immediately swerved to the shoulder of the highway to avoid a collision. The truck driver also swerved to the shoulder to avoid an accident. They were still both racing to a head-on collision. Paul swerved back on the highway. The trucker did too! Just before the impact, the trucker swerved hard to the right. Paul crashed into the side of the truck, just behind the front door. Paul felt like he was wrapped in a cloud during the accident. He was not even bumped or scratched during the great impact, yet the entire front of our car was pushed back into the motor block. The car came to a stop just over a hill on a busy highway. Cars and trucks were squealing to a stop to avoid hitting it. Paul jumped out of the car and ran up a hill on the edge of the highway. He sat down on that hill and began praising God for His love and protection. Then God spoke again. *Don't go to Tulsa.*

I won't!" Paul answered. "May I go to South Bend?" God's answer was a peace and assurance about going to South Bend.

When Paul was driven home later in a police car and told me all that had happened, I too praised God for His protection and leading.

I am so relieved," I told him. I didn't tell you, but I just felt as if something terrible would have happened if we had gone, either to us or the children."

"I felt the same way all day long," he said.

We still don't know why God said no, except that Paul possibly would have received invitations to preach in many Full Gospel churches, and it was not God's plan for our lives at that time. We don't really need to know God's reasons for His *Stop* and *Go* or *Yes* and *No*. Instead we just need to thank Him that He cares enough to stop us, in spite of our stubborn wills.

The next time He would speak to us, it would be to tell us to go when we didn't want to!

15

Whatsoever ye do, do all to the glory of God.
(I Corinthians 10:31)

Paul called Billy Walker, the preacher who had spoken to him in the middle of his message in the Toledo Sports Arena, and invited him to preach in a school auditorium in Muskegon. Paul offered to set up and advertise the meetings and provide the music.

Billy Walker accepted the invitation and we went to work. We rented the auditorium, ordered and hung five-hundred posters, passed out thousands of fliers, and paid for radio and newspaper ads. The auditorium was packed with people. Billy preached and ministered to the people and we had a tremendous meeting. The Lord moved among His people, and many lives were changed and empowered for service as a result of God touching them during those meetings.

When the meetings were over, Billy asked Paul if he would set up meetings for him all over the state of Michigan, and if we would go with him to provide the music. We prayed about it, and knew God was leading us to accept this responsibility. Neither Paul nor I wanted to go. Paul was holding revival crusades himself and seeing tremendous results. I had seven children to care for and did not want to leave any of them, especially my new Elizabeth.

Then God reminded Paul of the song he had made part of his life while he was being called into the ministry:

Jesus, Use me,
Please Lord, don't refuse me.
Surely there's a work that I can do.
And even though it's humble
Help my will to crumble.
Though the cost be great
I'll work for You.

God reminded me of the promise I had made to Him two years earlier: "Even if it means leaving my children in your care, Lord, I will give my life wholly to you." Now He was putting my promise to the test, and I didn't like the direction in which He was leading. God reminded me too of His warning, *"He that loveth son or daughter more than me is not worthy of me"* (Matthew 10:37).

We obeyed God's call.

We began to set up meetings all over the state of Michigan, traveling every Tuesday through Sunday for four consecutive weeks, taking a one week break, and then beginning another four weeks of travel. God provided very capable and loving Christian couples who took excellent care of our children on alternate weeks. We took at least one child with us, and often two or three.

Billy's ministry was to the Christians, and God worked through him to set many Christians aflame with the power of God. He reproved, rebuked and exhorted backslidden and powerless Christians fearlessly. There were tremendous services wherever we went.

Paul knew he was in the will of God, but he was restless. His main ministry was to the lost. Billy's entire ministry was to the saved. We didn't realize then an important truth God taught us through working with Billy. There is a fivefold ministry the Holy Spirit uses in the body of Christ to bring the saints to perfection. (See Ephesians 4:11-16)

1. Apostles
2. Prophets
3. Evangelists
4. Pastors
5. Teachers

The Bible says, *"Are all apostles? are all prophets? are all teachers? are all workers of miracles?"* (I Corinthians 12:29).

The apostle Peter ministered to the Jews. The apostle Paul ministered to the Gentiles. Together each member of the body of Christ, placed where the Holy Spirit places him, will fulfill the work God wants done on earth.

There is a ministry to sinners and a ministry to Christians. The end result of both is that souls will be saved. When the Christians are revived and set aflame for God, they will win souls to the Lord (II Corinthians 5:18-20).

Paul worked hard setting up those meetings. He had faithful advance teams go into a city before us to hang posters. He set up radio interviews for Billy. He appointed ushers. We arrived at the auditoriums early and set up the equipment. I took care of all of the finances, played the organ for the meetings, and sang special music with Paul.

At one service, while Paul was sitting offstage watching the tape recorder go around while recording Billy's sermon, he was feeling useless and confused. At that moment he heard the Lord say, *Sit up! Watch that tape recorder! This is a ministry. Many people will listen to these tapes, and they need to be good quality recordings. If you can't be obedient and faithful in this, how can I use you in anything greater?*

Paul sat up straight and looked at the recording level dial. From that night on, he began to watch that tape recorder as unto the Lord, doing the very best job he could do, for both Billy, a servant of the Lord, and the Lord Himself.

We often carried a playpen from auditorium to auditorium and kept Debbie backstage. She wasn't always good. One night she began hollering from her playpen, situated out of sight of the congregation, "Shut up, Billy! Shut up, Billy!" She was just over one year old, but had apparently felt that his sermon was far too long that night!

In Jackson, Michigan, we discovered we had to hire union electricians to sit through all the services, just to turn the lights on when we arrived and off when we left. They earned their wages by coloring in color books and reading Mother Goose and children's Bible stories to Janet and Judy backstage.

We were all packed in the car and ready to leave Alpena after the meetings were over, when God spoke to Paul, *The custodian needs me.*

Paul turned to me, "Wait just a few minutes," he said, and got out of the car and knocked on the already locked school door.

The custodian let him in. "Did you forget something?"

"Yes, I surely did," Paul answered, and before he returned to the car, that custodian had knelt in the school and received Christ as his personal Savior.

We enjoyed working with Billy and his wife, Beverly. They both were dedicated Christians who served the Lord sincerely with all the strength they had. We never saw either of them do or say anything that would bring reproach to the name of the Lord.

One afternoon between the morning and evening services at Port Huron, Michigan, I was called into the armory auditorium for a telephone call. I learned that Kathy, who was eleven years old at the time, had been injured in a bicycle accident. She had been racing down a hill on a sidewalk, hit a stone, and had flown over the handlebars and landed on her chin. I would find out later that she had broken both jaws, cut her chin, knocked out her only two remaining baby teeth, and would require eleven stitches to sew up a cut in her tongue.

"Take her immediately to the hospital," I told the mother who was at our home. I will call back in a few minutes and tell you when we will be home."

I prayed for Kathy and asked the Lord if I could go home immediately.

Immediately after the service, was His answer. Then He gave me a strength, a peace, and an assurance that Kathy would be all right. I could sing praises to Him in the meeting that evening with my daughter injured in a hospital on the other side of the state, because I knew God could care for her much better than I could, and I knew He was right in the hospital room with her.

We arrived at the hospital late that night, and then Paul returned to Port Huron. Kathy was transferred to a hospital in Muskegon for surgery the following morning. While I was waiting for Kathy to come out of surgery, the Lord released me from all the traveling I had done. I didn't know how He was going to work it all out but I knew my traveling was over for now. I was so relieved that I wanted to sing praises to God in the surgery department's waiting room of a Catholic hospital. I could be a full-time mother again!

"Father," I prayed, "I don't know what you are going to do with Paul and Billy, but I thank you for letting me stay home with my children again."

Paul came home from Port Huron the following Sunday evening. The people there had been wonderful. They had prayed earnestly for Kathy, had sent cards to her, and had given Paul money to help with the extra expenses we had.

The first thing Paul said when he arrived home was, I am going to tell Billy I can't work with him any more. The Lord has shown me that we have finished what He has wanted us to do in Michigan with Billy. Billy wants to go on to England and Canada, and he wants us to go with him, but our call was only to go to cities in Michigan with him. We have faithfully done that.

"God also showed me," he continued, "that I am to work now in the ministry He has called me to—winning souls. While I was in Port Huron, a young lady began sobbing toward the end of the service. She got louder and louder, until Billy finally told me to go quiet her down. I went to her and asked her what the problem was. She cried, "I want to get saved!" I went back to the front and made an altar out of a row of chairs and invited anyone who wanted to receive Christ to come up front. The altar was filled with people almost immediately and they were repenting of their sins. I knew right then that I could not go on without seeing souls saved, and God flooded me with a wonderful peace and assurance that I had finished the job He had called me to do!"

We didn't know where God would lead us now, but we did know we would in some way be involved in winning souls!

16

Whosoever heareth the sound of the trumpet, and taketh not warning; if the sword come, and take him away, his blood shall be upon his own head. But if the watchman see the sword come, and blow not the trumpet, and the people be not warned; if the sword come, and take any person from among them, he is taken away in his iniquity, but his blood will I require at the watchman's hand.
(Ezekiel 33:4, 6)

We formed a nonprofit ecclesiastical organization, registered by the state of Michigan and recognized by the United States government. We named it *Michigan for Christ*, because our prayer was that the people of Michigan, a cold state both physically and spiritually, would turn to Jesus Christ.

An accountant who helped us set up our bookkeeping system recommended his lawyer from Fremont, Michigan to us. The lawyer helped us organize *Michigan for Christ* and never charged us for all his work. When he finished, we were set up to establish churches, missions, schools, orphanages, etc.—both in the United States and overseas. His vision was bigger than ours!

One night I couldn't sleep because Paul's message on Bible prophecy continued to ring through my mind. I finally got up and wrote what I thought was to be a tract on it. The next morning when Paul read it, he said, "Get it printed. It will be good to have something to leave for the people with all these Scripture verses on the last days in it." Some friends of ours read it. "It's good! Get it printed," they advised. But I didn't type it up for the printers. About four months passed. "I just don't feel like the time is right," I told Paul when he asked why I didn't get it printed.

Then I heard the Lord speak. *You are to publish a monthly paper. This is the first article.* The *Sound of the Trumpet* was born in January, 1972. It began with a mailing list of sixteen hundred names we had collected wherever we had ministered. We had no idea why we were collecting names, except that every time we saw a preacher friend from Ohio named George, he would say, "Paul, collect names of the people you meet. You will need them some day."

"Why?" Paul would ask him.

"You will be glad you did!" he would answer.

The next time we would see George, he would ask, "Are you collecting names?"

"No," we would laugh.

"I am telling you—collect names!"

Because of George's insistence, we collected names. When the first issue of *Sound of the Trumpet* was published, we had sixteen hundred families to send it to!

Within four and a half years of monthly publication, we had twenty thousand families on our mailing list, and the *Sound of the Trumpet* was mailed into every state of the United States and twenty-seven foreign countries.

There were many times during those years when I never would have kept the paper going if I hadn't been sure it had been ordained of God. The majority of the responsibility for the paper fell upon me. I wrote Paul's messages down, prepared them for the printer, proofread all the material, did the book work, and answered hundreds of letters every week. Many times when I was swamped with office work, the care of the home and children, packing to leave for another revival meeting, and facing a deadline for the next issue, God would give me supernatural strength to keep going. He also sent a wonderful Christian couple who spent most of their free time helping to keep the mailing list up-to-date. Max and Karen worked without pay and without complaint, and made our load much lighter by their dedication to the ministry of helps.

One young man from Ghana, West Africa, wrote that he bought meat in a market and it was wrapped in a *Sound of the Trumpet.* He received Jesus Christ into his life as a result of his meat wrapper!

Many were saved and many Christians were blessed through the paper, and that made it worth the time it cost. As soon as it was printed, Paul would take the responsibility of getting the thousands of papers addressed and mailed.

One day we had the papers all ready to mail, but we lacked $100 to pay the postage. We prayed about it and the Lord said, *Write the check for the postage.* "But, Lord, we don't have money in the bank to cover it!" *Write the check.*

We wrote the check and took the papers to the post office and mailed them. I looked away from the postmaster as I handed him the check. Then we went over to our post office box and took out one letter. It contained $100 from a church in Muskegon Heights. We had dragged ourselves into the post office, but we almost floated out!

One morning Paul told me, "God wants us to start mailing a special salvation issue of *Sound of the Trumpet* into every home in towns and cities of Michigan."

"What? Are you *sure*?" I questioned. "How do we get the names and addresses?"

"I don't know," he answered. "Probably from telephone books."

I could see a room full of hundreds of telephone books and thousands of papers, and hear children crying in the background and picture me sitting in the middle of the room, bleary-eyed, copying addresses. My vision was a nightmare!

Paul went to the post office. "How do advertisers mail their literature into homes? Where do they get the addresses?" he asked.

"They have big mailing lists, I suppose," the postmaster answered. "Why?"

"What about politicians? How do they do it?"

"Well—there is a place we give addresses to. Come back later, and I will see if I can locate their address."

Paul came home later with the name of an addressing firm in Detroit. "Yes, we have every address in Michigan. . . in the whole United States, as a matter of fact. You can bring some papers down and we will address them for you. Your cost will be eight dollars for one thousand papers."

We printed up a special issue of *Sound of the Trumpet* with every article aimed at winning lost souls to Jesus Christ. As soon as they were printed, we took them to Detroit to have them addressed to homes in several towns, cities, and entire counties in Michigan. That was the first trip of many we made to Detroit, with our car loaded full of papers. The total cost of one salvation paper, including printing, addressing, and mailing, was only five and one-half cents. Many Christians paid to have the towns they lived in saturated with the gospel message. Some Christians paid to saturate entire counties.

One woman wrote us from Monroe, Michigan. "I can't witness to people well, because I am totally deaf. But this is a way I can witness. I want to send the gospel message into every home in this city." And she did.

While I worked on the papers, Paul took on another soul-winning project. This one would take him right to jail!

17

I was in prison, and ye came unto me. Then shall the righteous answer him (Jesus) saying, Lord, when saw we thee... in prison, and came unto thee? And the King shall answer and say unto them, Verily I say unto you, In as much as ye have done it unto one of the least of these my brethren, ye have done it unto me. (Matthew 25:36-40)

Paul received a telephone call one day from an anxious mother who was pleading with him to visit her son in the county jail. Paul went to visit the young man, and while he was there, God gave him a burden for the men locked in jail. He asked the sheriff if he could hold a service in the jail once a week. The sheriff's consent was just the beginning of some exciting times for Paul and some friends who went with him into the jail.

The sheriff gave Paul the ring of keys and an empty cell for conducting services. "Just don't unlock those two first cells!" he cautioned. "Those guys might give you trouble."

Paul went from cell to cell, unlocking the doors and saying, "Come on, guys. Follow me." The prisoners looked at Paul's size, and wondering if he was a detective, new cop or what, followed him into the big cell. They found out who he was. They were locked in an old-fashioned revival meeting by the time they discovered he was a preacher!

Paul was elated! He had a captive audience! He preached a sermon on *"God's Jail."* He told those men that the jail they were in was peanuts, compared to the jail they were going to be transferred to at their death.

"You think this jail is bad? Listen to this! You are on your way to a jail with no lights, no beds, no food, no water. The worst lunatics and criminals this world has ever produced are there. It is a combination of the worst jail and the worst insane asylum you can even imagine. Its inmates spend their time screaming, wailing, and gnashing their teeth. Your buddies might be sent there too, but they will be no company to you."

"One man, a very wealthy businessman, went there a few thousand years ago. He said, 'Warn my brothers to confess their crimes and plead for mercy from their Judge, so they will not have to come here. It's terrible here. It's unbearably hot. I have begged for just one drop of water, but there is no one to even listen to me. There is no water here.' He had five brothers, but he wasn't looking forward to being reunited with them. He wanted them spared from this jail at all costs." (See Luke 16:19-31.)

"I don't know if his brothers went there or not. But I do know one thing. That rich man is still there, in torment, begging for one drop of water. No one who goes there ever gets out again."

Paul looked straight at the men. *"You* have been sentenced to this jail. You have broken God's laws, and this is your judgment—God's jail. Hell. Not just for life. Forever."

"There is only one way to change your sentence. That way is Jesus Christ. He is God. He came to earth as a man like yourself. He was born into the human race just so He could pay for your sins and crimes with His own blood. His death and resurrection set you free. But you have a responsibility now to see that your sentence is lifted."

"Go to God, your Creator. He is the Father of Jesus. Plead guilty. Tell Him you are a sinner. Admit that you have broken His laws. Thank Him for His mercy to you. He allowed His only son to die an agonizing death so you can be set free."

"Plead for His mercy and He will pardon you. He is the kindest, most merciful judge you will ever stand before. He has compassion and love. He has never refused a single case. He has pardoned every single person who has come before Him and asked for His mercy, love and forgiveness and accepted His Son's payment for their sins. It is the only way you can be set free and have your sentence lifted. But you have to do it now. You can't wait until you die and expect mercy. It will be too late then. You will be sentenced forever to hell —*God's jail.*"

Men fell on their knees in that cell and repented of their sins that night. Angels rejoiced as sinners were saved.

Paul gave the men Bibles and promised to return the following week. One of the best revival meetings Paul ever had was in that jail cell.

One night, Paul received permission from the sheriff to take one of the prisoners to a river to be baptized. All went well, except that a large fish (probably sent by the devil) swam up and bit the prisoner's foot just before he was immersed!

During one service, a prisoner the men called "Big John" began to scream and tear at his chest in obvious torment. Paul commanded the devil in him to come out, and after a few torturous minutes, the devil left Big John's body. Later he confided to Paul that he began to scream while Paul was preaching because he felt like there was a giant fish hook within him, tearing at him. As Paul commanded the devil to leave, Big John said the "hook" tore upward until it left through the top of his head.

Devils not only inhabited people two thousand years ago, while Jesus walked the earth. They still inhabit people today.

Big John read his Bible and testified to God's goodness constantly in the jail after that night. One day when Paul entered the jail, the sheriff said, "Come here, I want to show you something." Tacked on the wall in his office was a letter to the sheriff from the prisoners, thanking him for letting the big preacher hold services. "Big John" was the first signature on the letter.

The sheriffs department called Paul about supper time one evening and asked him if he would come right down to the jail.

"We have an uncontrollable prisoner," they told him when he arrived, as they led him to a cell. A young man was screaming and banging his head on the wall. A doctor and the prosecuting attorney were standing with the deputy, authorizing the department to commit him to a mental institution.

"He keeps calling for the priest," the deputy said. "Go on in and see what you can do with him. "

The prisoner eyed Paul suspiciously when he entered the cell. "Are you a priest?" he asked him.

"I am a preacher," Paul answered.

"Come here then."

Paul walked closer to him. "Listen, priest," he whispered, "I'm not nuts. But I am not going to the state prison where they want to take me. I have been there. It's terrible. I will kill myself first. I will bang my head until it breaks before I will go back to that prison. "

The deputy called to Paul, "We are taking him to the hospital in Kalamazoo. He has calmed down since you arrived, and we want to keep him calm. We want you to ride with him in the back of the car. "

They wrapped their prisoner in a straightjacket and put him and Paul in the caged back seat of the sheriffs car. Paul sat with the "mad man" as the car raced at breakneck speed to deliver its passenger to the insane asylum.

Isn't it amazing that a perfectly healthy young man would go to such extreme measures to escape going to one of Michigan's jails, when millions of people go through life unconcerned that they are destined to spend their eternity in hell?

18

God is our refuge and strength, a very present help in trouble. (Psalm 46:1)

One morning, Paul's Uncle Ivan knocked on our door. Paul had led him to the Lord in our living room shortly after we had moved to Hart.

Uncle Ivan and Paul chatted for a while, and then Uncle Ivan said, "How are you coming on fixing up the Thunderbird you bought? I know where there is one like it, if you need parts."

A couple of minutes later they were leaving for Hart to look at the car.

An hour later they returned, and Paul hadn't even closed the door before he was yelling, "Carolyn! Where are you? Come here quick!"

I went to see what was wrong, and he said, "Wait till you see it! It's beautiful! I think we can buy it! It's just huge! There must be about thirty bedrooms, ten bathrooms. It's all brick...!"

"What are you talking about?" I interrupted. "I thought you went to see a car!"

"Yes, but this building is just across the road from where the car is. It was a county hospital. It's empty now. Uncle Ivan knows the man who bought it from the county. We just went through it. It's a fantastic building!

101

We could use it for the Lord's work...a church, offices, Christians retreats, our house...everything! Come on, I will show it to you!"

"Will the owner mind if we go through it?" I asked.

"No, no. It's okay. We don't need a key."

Just before we arrived at the building, Paul warned me, "It will need some fixing up."

We drove up to a huge, U-shaped brick building in a beautiful setting of maple and cedar trees. We went to the side porch. No wonder we didn't need a key. The door was laying flat on the porch, and a screen door was swinging in the wind. We walked into a hall, 105 feet long. Paul was right. It was huge. There were all kinds of bedrooms and bathrooms, and many huge extra rooms we could use for offices, living and dining rooms and kitchens.

The only things he had failed to mention were that sixty-five windows were smashed on the floors, lawn and porches; the light fixtures had been pulled from their sockets and were hanging dismally. The bathtubs and sinks were cracked and laying on the floor in the halls or bathrooms; there were huge holes in the walls and ceilings. There was enough trash, broken glass and filth strewn around to fill two trailers! Birds were flying through the rooms. We surprised a couple of squirrels who thought they had the place to themselves.

"Wait until you see the upstairs," Paul said excitedly.

I could hardly wait. I dragged up after him and followed him into the open second floor.

"Be careful!" he shouted. "Watch where you step!"

I looked down at the floor. Floor? There wasn't one!

We were walking on boards laid across the ceiling rafters of the floor below.

I wasn't impressed.

Then we went down to the full basement. Rooms and more rooms. Dirty rooms.

"Isn't it something?" Paul asked. "A little work..."

He went to see the owner. While Paul was talking to the elderly man, the Holy Spirit talked to Paul.

The building is nothing compared to this man's soul. Tell him about Jesus. It doesn't matter if he gets angry and throws you out. He is more important than a building. His soul is more important to me than the entire world!

Paul witnessed to the man and introduced him to Jesus Christ. The gentleman said he would consider what Paul had said about Christ, but did not wish to make a decision that evening.

Paul then asked him about the building, and discovered he could buy it for $12,500 on a land contract, with no money down, and payments of fifty dollars a month. He was elated. I couldn't believe we were going to undertake such a project. But during the next few days, I began to visualize the finished building and the potential it had, and I began to get excited too.

Everyone we talked to about purchasing it said we would be crazy to buy it. A realtor said, "You are foolish to even consider it. The water has been off for eight years. Is there water? The furnace has not been lit for eight years. Does it work? Do you have any idea what it will cost to repair and redecorate a place of twenty thousand square feet? Paul, you would be crazy to buy it!"

103

So...we bought it!

We put our house up for sale and it sold right away, leaving us with a profit to begin work on what we began to call "*the castle*." Nothing about it resembled a castle except its size.

The first thing we did was remove trailer loads of dirt and trash. Then we fixed up one bedroom in the main hall. It turned out beautiful. It looked rather odd though, to go through this huge building, every room and hall a disaster, and then to see one lone room beautifully painted, furnished, nice drapes at the windows, the bed neatly made, a floral arrangement on the dresser, and pictures on the walls! But it made us realize we really could redo this place—one room at a time.

The next thing we had to fix was the wing we would use to live in. Its hall was seventy feet long. There was no kitchen, but there was a large room we could make into a kitchen and dining room. We could look through a hole in our potential living room and see the sky! We had only a few weeks before we had to vacate our house for the new owner.

We went to a wallpaper store in Muskegon that we had never been in. We told the manager what we had bought. "I have a lot of rolls of perfectly good wallpaper in stock," Jerry said. "It is not pre-pasted though, and everyone wants pre-pasted paper. It sells for five to twelve dollars a single roll. I will let you have it for thirty-five cents a roll!"

We returned home with our car fall of beautiful wallpaper and our hearts full of praise.

A Christian friend, whose husband was a professional painter, said, "My husband has all kinds of paint in our back room. The cans have been partially used, but there is enough paint there that we can mix together and come up with some beautiful colors."

That is the way our buying the materials went. Every time we needed something, God would lead us to someone or lead someone to us who had a surplus of that particular thing. We purchased excellent dry wall for less than most lumber companies were paying for it.

Paul woke up one morning with a groan. "This is the day."

"For what?" I asked.

"This is the day we turn the water on for the first time in eight years— if there is water."

"Oh, I am sure it will work fine," I assured him.

There was water! The castle had so many broken water pipes that water was spraying and spurting and pouring all over the building.

"Turn it off! Turn it off!" Paul yelled as he surveyed the fountains.

Another day Paul turned the huge furnace on. The furnace room filled with billowing smoke and the furnace emitted a number of threatening sounding puffs. Paul discovered the chimney was plugged about eight feet deep with various debris—bird nests, squirrel nests, and all kinds of strange things that kept the smoke from escaping.

The part of the castle we would live in was finally finished. It turned out so beautiful that people who hadn't seen it before we redecorated it couldn't believe it had once looked like the rest of the castle. Our living room was huge, and it had twelve windows, each one with a nice view. We moved in on Christmas Eve, during the worst blizzard of the year.

On New Year's Eve, we had a service for our friends in the Lord. We had planned to sing and praise God for the first hour, have fellowship and refreshments the second hour, and spend the final hour of the old year with a communion service and prayer for a fresh anointing from God for the coming year.

At about seven o'clock we discovered we had no water. Paul went across the road and waded through deep snow to go down a huge, steep hill to the artesian well.

"The pump quit working," he announced when he returned. He called several people and finally located the owner of a well-drilling business at his home. "Bring your pump over," he said. "I will see if I can fix it."

People were arriving for the service. Paul invited a few men to accompany him over the hill to haul the pump up on a toboggan. Then they took it to Walkerville to get it repaired.

I looked at the people congregated together. "Could one of you men lead in some songs and testimonies?" I asked. Don barely began the first song when we heard an explosion. "What was that?" we all asked in unison.

The men all left and went to the basement. One came back to tell us the furnace had exploded and they were trying to fix it. By the time they had taken the furnace apart, repaired it, put it back together again, and were black with soot, the other men were trudging up the hill, after installing the repaired pump, white with snow.

At midnight, we were all greatly relieved to see the old year go!

Our friends left, and we fell exhausted into bed. About an hour later, we woke up. We were cold. "Now what?" Paul mumbled.

"We are out of fuel oil," he said a little later. We had bought some fuel oil for our six thousand gallon underground tank, but apparently not enough. Paul finally located our fuel oil man at a New Year's party. At three o'clock in the morning, he arrived with his truck to give us fuel oil, singing drunkenly.

What a night!

There were two New Year's Eves we would never forget. One was a joyful occasion, for we welcomed our third child, Dennis, into our family.

The other was our first one in the castle.

Two weeks later, our eighth (and final) child, beautiful little Suzanne Lisa, was born.

19

Cast thy burden upon the Lord, and he shall sustain thee. (Psalm 55:22)

Paul decided to make the entire second floor of the castle into a church auditorium. What an undertaking it was! He hired one carpenter, and Norm and Paul went to work.

During the next five months, we kept going on God's strength alone. We worked about seventeen hours a day. We had set May 26, the Friday of Memorial Day weekend, as our opening day. All we had to do before then was remodel and redecorate every inch of a twenty thousand square foot building. In our spare time, we had to keep our monthly publication going and care for our eight children. Our oldest child, Kathy, was ten at the time. Also we had services twice a week in the castle and Paul accepted invitations for many one, two or three day revival meetings and concerts in cities across Michigan!

We advertised our grand opening in our *Sound of the Trumpet*, announced our summer and fall schedule of speakers, and invited people to come and stay for the weekend.

It was May 24. The last five months had been something!

The church was finished, and it was beautiful. A city crane had come out in a rainstorm and lifted up the huge rolls of carpeting through an upstairs window. Somehow Paul had managed to get the pews upstairs by removing windows and hoisting them over stair casings. The grand piano had been lugged upstairs and set in place.

There were two sets of stairs inside the castle, but the castle needed another set of stairs going directly from the outside up to the church. Paul and Norm had never made a set of stairs, but they figured they could do it as well as anybody. The first set ended up being used as truck racks. Paul hadn't realized how peculiar his truck looked until he was on his way to Muskegon for supplies one day. A policeman came up beside him and ordered him off the road.

"Now what?" Paul wondered. "I wasn't speeding."

The policeman came up to the window.

"License."

Paul gave it to him.

He glanced at it, handed it back, then pointed to Paul's unusual truck rack. "Was that supposed to be a set of stairs?"

"Yes," Paul answered him. "We built them wrong, so I am using them for a truck rack."

The policeman started laughing. "That's what I thought! Just had to know for sure," and he continued to stand there laughing. He finally noticed that Paul wasn't amused, so he said, "Well, thanks, Buddy. You made my day!" and still laughing and shaking his head, went back to his car.

Then there had been the day a truckload of dry wall was delivered. The truck drove into a steep snow bank, hit a buried curb, tipped up on its side, and dumped the entire load of supplies into the deep snow.

One day when Paul was exhausted, a truck arrived with another huge load of material. Paul groaned, realizing he had to unload it and lug it upstairs.

"Just a minute," he told the driver. He telephoned the high school. "How would you like to build up some muscles on your wrestling team?" he asked the coach.

A few minutes later, the wrestling team arrived. Within a short time, all the materials were off the truck and stacked neatly upstairs.

The room we had finished looked beautiful. A Christian contractor from Zeeland had arrived and built beautiful tables and benches in our cafeteria.

A few days before our opening, Paul hated to put down his hammer and leave for another one night revival meeting. We didn't know how we could possibly finish the building by Friday. He wondered if he should call the pastor and tell him we just couldn't make it. Then the Lord reminded him of a verse He has often reminded us of: "Seek ye first the kingdom of God, and his righteousness; and all these things shall be added unto you" (Matthew 6:33).

Oh, we hated leaving, but we had a tremendous meeting and many people responded to the gospel message. We returned home about midnight. The castle was all lit up. We went in and found a whole crew of Christian friends laughing and singing and working their hearts out. God had accomplished much more work by sending laborers in than we could have accomplished had we stayed home!

Now it was Thursday evening. Our first guests were scheduled to arrive about ten o'clock the following morning. The plumbers were still there, frantically trying to repair all the pipes. Paul had decided to make two men's restrooms out of one large one, and he had just chopped a huge hole in the wall to make a doorway. We women were frantically wallpapering the last rooms. We had our mops and buckets ready, waiting for water so we could scrub all the hall floors. The plumber had the water turned off.

At midnight, the plumber stood up and stretched. "Can't wrap it up tonight. Sorry. Gotta get some sleep."

We couldn't believe he was actually forsaking us, but we watched him walk out the door, away from the still broken pipes and our pleading faces. We continued working until four o'clock in the morning, then went home exhausted. At six o'clock in the morning, the plumber arrived. At eight o'clock we had water. At nine-thirty we finished our building. At nine forty-five our first guests arrived.

Three hundred people came to our first retreat. Our castle was packed. There were trailers and tents set up on our grounds, and the motels in Hart were filled.

It was the beginning of five solid months of weekend retreats. We provided two services a day on Friday, Saturday, and Sunday; two special children's services during the weekend; and three hours daily of personal counseling. And oh, yes...all the meals for all the people!

If we had thought we were busy before, we found out during the retreats we were just as busy now that the building was finished and the retreats had started!

We had some wonderful servants of God as speakers. We met many brothers and sisters in Christ and had sweet fellowship with them. We had some beautiful services. But when our last service closed on Sunday afternoon of October 14, 1973, we knew it was not only the last service of that week, but it was also the last service of our weekend retreats.

The people who came were Christian people. The speakers preached to their Christian congregation. We were not reaching lost souls through weekend retreats, and when souls were not being saved through our ministry, we felt like failures. God had called Paul not only to preach to the lukewarm Christians, but to win the lost.

We had some outstanding victories among the Christians though. Aggie, a registered nurse, had come from the Flint area. The final stages of leukemia were sapping the life from her body. She had been treated at Ford Hospital in Detroit, and had flown to Houston, Texas twice for a complete blood change. She had flown to Houston the third time to have her blood drained and her system flushed with a solution. The medical profession was doing all it could do to save her, but it was not enough. She returned to Flint and her veins collapsed. She had brain damage. She developed breast cancer, then stomach cancer. After an intern left the cobalt on her too long during one treatment, her intestines were badly burned. She was a beautiful woman of forty years old.

Aggie and her husband, Foy, arrived at one of our weekend retreats while Brother Leonard Ravenhill was our guest speaker. They asked Paul if he would pray for Aggie, and he told them he would pray for her the following morning.

That evening while Brother Ravenhill was speaking, Aggie crumpled up against her husband unconscious. Then she quit breathing. I was sitting directly behind them, and watched as her husband frantically gave her mouth-to-mouth resuscitation. People all around us were praying for her. She finally gasped and began breathing again.

The following morning, she and her husband met Paul in his office. Paul laid his hand on her head and rebuked the cancer in the name of Jesus, and prayed that she would be healed.

Aggie was instantly and completely healed. She went to her doctor on Monday morning. He ordered extensive testing to be done and pronounced her cancer completely gone. There was no more brain damage, no more stomach cancer, no more breast cancer, no more leukemia! Even the scars from her cobalt burns had vanished! All Aggie's diseases were gone because of Jesus! By His stripes, Aggie was gloriously healed!

But as wonderful as that miracle was, and as much as we praise God for His healing power, we longed to see and be part of souls being saved. That is the greater miracle...the dead being raised to newness of life as Christ reaches down and saves a soul!

We didn't know it then, but the following year we would see literally hundreds of souls find Jesus Christ as their Savior. And it would all begin by a visit from a Nazarene.

20

Bless the Lord, O my soul and all that is within me, bless his holy name. Bless the Lord, O my soul, and forget not all his benefits: Who forgiveth all thine iniquities; who healeth all thy diseases. (Psalm 103:1-3)

The superintendent of a Michigan district of the Nazarene churches called Paul one morning and made arrangements to come and talk with him. He had been a friend of Paul's family for years and had known Paul when he was a young boy.

He came to the castle and he and Paul talked about the work God had called Paul to do. Then the conversation drifted to the lukewarm, stale condition of the churches.

"Paul, come into our churches and preach. We need a revival. If God doesn't give the Nazarene church a revival, we will die the way many other denominations have died. They used to be on fire for God and are now just powerless social groups in our communities. I don't want to see that happen to our Nazarene churches! We need to have the power of God move again in our churches!"

"Come to our annual camp meeting. I will introduce you to our pastors and recommend that they invite you to their churches."

We went to the camp meeting, where Paul was introduced as an evangelist. He talked to the pastors for only about five minutes, but God anointed his words. Before he returned to his seat, he had revival meetings booked.

And they were literally revival meetings. Many times we label evangelistic crusades revival meetings, even though there is no revival. But God blessed those meetings beyond what we could have even hoped for.

We mailed a special salvation issue of *Sound of the Trumpet* into every home in the city or county we were going to, and announced in the issue our coming meetings and invited everyone to come. People came! Churches were packed.

God blessed Paul's sermons, and the Word of God began to do its work. It went out as a sword and cracked open hard shells and exposed people for what they were.

The altars were lined with weeping people. Backsliders wept their way back to God. Many Christians who had never testified at work or at school began to open their mouths for Christ and proclaim Him as Savior, Lord, and coming King. People who had wronged or robbed others made restitution. Feuds and bitter feelings were confessed, forgiven and forgotten.

When love and peace were restored to a church, the blessings of God returned to it. Why would God have blessed a church full of bickering members? The beams had to be cast out of the eye of the church before it could work on the mote in the eye of the world! Jesus said, *"By this shall all men know that ye are my disciples, if ye have love one to another"* (John 13:35).

Paul urged the church members to bring the lost into the meetings. He preached to them, and countless lost people found new hope and a new life in Christ. One young man ran down the aisle during the altar call, leaped up on the platform, and grabbed and hugged Paul while he wept his way to Christ.

The next evening, he led his weeping wife to the altar, and he was able to lead her to Jesus.

One dignified, middle-aged wealthy businessman wanted to go forward during the altar call. He was with his wife and another couple, and he was sitting on the inside of the pew. He tried and tried unsuccessfully to get past his wife. She stood unyielding and blocked his way to the aisle. She wasn't going to let him embarrass her by going to an altar to pray! He finally gave up trying that route. He stood on the pew, then onto the tops of the pew in front of him, and walking from pew top to pew top, made it to the front of the church, where he knelt and found Christ. His wife probably would have been much less mortified if she had let him pass in front of her!

One husky young man who had a reputation at the local bars as a rough customer because of his involvement in many fights was gloriously saved. He wept like a baby, as he was born again into the family of God.

During an altar call in Paul's home church in Alanson, Michigan, the lights suddenly went out and the organ and microphone died. The electricity had gone out in a severe thunderstorm. It was pitch black. While Paul's Aunt Naomi found her way to the front to light a candle, Paul continued with his altar call, not hesitating even a second. "Just as quickly as the lights went off in this church, your life could go out and you could find yourself in the blackness of eternity, on your way to an appointment with God. *'It is appointed unto men once to die, but after this the judgment.'* (Hebrews 9:27) Are you ready to face God with an account of your life?"

When the lights came on a few minutes later, the altar was filled and people all over the church were kneeling at their seats, weeping and praying.

Paul taught on water baptism during the Sunday school hour in one country church. Twenty people wanted to be baptized. The preacher got Paul off to one side. "Paul, what shall I do? I can't baptize these people; I have never been baptized myself!"

"Fine," Paul answered. "I will baptize you, then you baptize them."

"I want to be baptized," the pastor answered, "especially after hearing your teaching today from the Word of God. But what will my people think?"

"Tell them," Paul answered, "to follow you as you lead them in water baptism."

He did, and that afternoon we drove into the country and along the driveway of a farmhouse. We walked a short distance behind the house, across some rolling hills. Coming to a bank, we looked below us to a beautiful, winding river.

Twenty people went down the bank and into the river to be baptized on that beautiful Sunday afternoon. The pastor was the first one to wade to the middle of the river, leading his people into obedience to God's Word. He reached the center and looked back up the hill. He couldn't believe his eyes. A great crowd of people stood on the hill watching. He didn't know who many of them were. He had never seen them before and had no idea how they knew about the baptism. Behind him, a canoe paddled to a stop and waited. God had brought people to watch as each child of God went into the water, testifying that they had died to their old way of life and wished to bury it, and came up out of the water, showing themselves to be alive unto God.

That evening, after several others found Christ at the altar, the pastor and Paul prayed for those who needed God's healing touch. Over fifty people received instant healing. Deaf ears were opened, cataracts vanished, vertebrae were put back in place, a crooked arm was straightened, heart conditions were healed. People were starved for God, and when He reached down and met their needs, they responded by praising and magnifying His name. Oh, what beautiful times of praise followed both the salvations and the healings!

God cannot break His Word. He says, *"It pleased God by the foolishness of preaching to save them that believe. For the preaching of the cross is to them that perish foolishness; but unto us which are saved it is the power of God"* (I Corinthians 1:21, 18). God's Word works today. When the preaching of the cross is preached with the anointing of the Holy Spirit, men are saved.

God has said, *"These signs shall follow them that believe...they shall lay hands on the sick, and they shall recover. And the prayer of faith shall save the sick, and the Lord shall raise him up"* (Mark 16:17-18, James 5:15).

All we need to do is obey the Word of God. God will do the rest. Preach the cross; men will be saved. Lay hands on the sick; men will be healed. The Bible is a fresh Word, alive with the breath of God, and we can live by every word of it today.

Don't let mere men cause you by their lengthy explanations of the Bible to doubt the Word of God. The devil has been making men doubt God's Word from the very beginning. He said to Eve, after God had told her she would die if she ate the forbidden fruit, *"Yea, hath God said? . . . Ye shall not surely die"* (Genesis 3:1, 4).

The Bible says, *"Let God be true, but every man a liar"* (Romans 3:4). *"God is not a man, that he should lie...hath he said, and shall he not do it? or hath he spoken, and shall he not make it good?"* (Numbers 23:19).

If Christians today just began believing the Bible and acting on it, we would see a revival in our churches that would shake the world for Christ! We discovered when we put the Bible to the test and simply did what it said to do, God always blessed with wonderful results.

We traveled from one end of Michigan to the other, holding meetings in small country churches, old city churches, modern suburban churches, churches of one-hundred members, and churches of twenty-seven hundred members. We went wherever doors opened to us, not only in Michigan, but also in Florida, West Virginia, Virginia, Indiana, Wisconsin, and New Mexico.

Our meetings usually lasted Wednesday through Sunday, and sometimes only Friday through Sunday. We always took two, three, or four of our children with us. After the final Sunday service, we would load up our van with our organ, sound equipment, saxophone, electric piano and children, and drive all night to get home as soon as possible so our children wouldn't miss too much school. We missed a boat from Wisconsin to Michigan after one Sunday evening service, and had to drive north in Wisconsin to catch another one. We sat up until four-thirty the next morning waiting for the boat to be loaded, then we finally got on board. We arrived in Michigan at 7:30 A.M. and an hour later, tumbled into our castle.

We were greeted with, "Did you have a nice vacation?"

During the one or two days we were home before our next meetings, we would frantically race to the printers to proofread another copy of *Sound of the Trumpet*, or to Detroit with a van load of papers that needed to be addressed. We would gather up our mail and try to restore order to the office work that had piled up in our absence. We would hastily unpack suitcases and repack them with clothes for a different group of children, and then we would be off for another state, another church.

We took all eight children to one meeting. We couldn't bear to leave any of them, so we just loaded them all in the van and headed for a city in Michigan. We spread out sleeping bags in two adjoining motel rooms, and it all worked out pretty well except when Paul wanted silence so he could study. We didn't try that again!

We had some precious times with our children then, even though it was a hectic way of life. We could spend more time with each child individually. Mike and Elizabeth went to Florida with us, and, for Mike's sake, we stopped in Kentucky long enough to take him through a cave. I wasn't happy at all about being underground, and was relieved to see daylight again, but it was an experience Mike really enjoyed.

We could hardly tear Dennis and Kathy away from New Mexico. They made new friends there, and didn't want to leave them.

Janet and Judy loved the boat trip across Lake Michigan. Suzy despised it, and let us know she did, in no uncertain screams!

I loved West Virginia. We were at the highest point in the Appalachian Mountains, and I considered it closest to heaven. Paul was sick the whole time we were there and didn't recover until he reached lowland again.

Debbie enjoyed going along wherever it was, as long as she was with Mom and Dad.

Somehow we managed to keep the revival meetings going, our family going, and our monthly paper going. Often I spent much of my time in various motel rooms answering hundreds of letters and typing articles for the *Sound of the Trumpet*.

At home while we were gone, Max and Karen, a dedicated Christian couple, moved right into the castle with their two children to take care of our children. On Fridays, Paul's parents arrived from two hundred miles away to spend the weekend spoiling our kids. They would leave for home on Sunday afternoon, and Max and Karen would take over again until we arrived.

It was a busy and often chaotic way of life for all of us, but the results of the meetings kept us going.

At one dying church, Paul asked the pastor what he was doing in his area to reach lost souls.

"Nothing. Can't reach the ones around here," was his answer. "These people are rough! You just don't know what this place is like!"

"Let's try," Paul said.

The preacher reluctantly agreed to try going visiting with him the next day. The following morning, the pastor was all smiles. "Got just the one for you to call on," he greeted Paul. "A farmer. A *mean* farmer. He hates church. He doesn't like Christians. He *really* doesn't like preachers!"

"Great! I was raised on a farm," was Paul's answer.

They found the farmer in his barn. Paul waded through manure, chatting with him about his farm and relating some of his own experiences on the farm.

He followed the farmer from chore to chore, and the pastor trailed behind them. The farmer finally realized he couldn't shake his two visitors, so he invited them into his house. "I didn't come to talk to you about church," Paul began. "I came to talk to you about Jesus."

Paul led that "mean farmer" and his wife to Jesus. The couple knelt in their living room and gave their hearts and what remained of their lives to Christ. They rose to their feet radiant, new people in the Lord, their past sins washed away in the blood of Christ.

That evening they were not only in church, but they brought along a car full of friends and relatives. Every service they were in church, rejoicing in their new life. Some of their family and friends also found Christ.

The pastor was dumbfounded. "It works. It really works," he said, shaking his head.

Sometimes Christians act as if the gospel is bad news they are obligated to deliver, rather than the life giving good news we have the privilege to offer!

In one town, the church was filled beyond capacity, so the meetings were transferred to the school auditorium. On Sunday, the Methodist church closed its doors and joined the revival meeting.

One group of teenagers slipped into the back. They were noisy and came to disturb the meeting. Paul rebuked them and they quieted down. At the altar call, a teen-age girl from the group was the first one to the altar. She could not pray. She could not even say the name, "Jesus." The devil had bound her through drugs and her search for happiness in the world of the occult. Paul commanded the devil to leave her body and she was set free to accept Christ. She was gloriously saved and began praising the name of Jesus...the same name that only moments earlier she could not even say.

That was just the beginning of a tremendous revival among the young people of that town. Many teenagers realized they had delved too far into the devil's kingdom. Only Jesus, who said He came to set the captives free, could help them. Paul cast out devils in the name of Jesus, and those young people found a greater power in Jesus than they had ever found in the occult.

After the final service in a church in Michigan's upper peninsula, a pastor leaped from the platform and, standing in front of his congregation, shouted, "Pentecost has come! If we ever go back from this to our dead ways, God help us!"

While we were in meetings in Jackson, Michigan, the prison chaplain of the Michigan State Prison contacted

Paul and invited him in to preach. It is the largest walled prison in the world and over six thousand prisoners are confined there.

At two o'clock one fall afternoon, over one hundred prisoners gathered in the chapel. Paul preached on "*God's Jail*" and over thirty-five prisoners came forward weeping, repented of their sins and received Jesus Christ into their hearts and lives.

At one nearly dead church, God swept through with the breath of life. Many people found Christ, and when those Christians who were part of the church discovered that God really does save and give new life to sinners, they were set on fire. Revival fires spread through the church and town.

The pastor's telephone rang constantly during the day with reports of victories among his people.

By the time Sunday evening arrived, the sick knew they would be healed. They had seen God move by His Spirit all week, and they didn't limit His power by their unbelief. They believed He could heal bodies as well as save souls. That evening, a deaf man heard for the first time in years. A blind lady received her sight. A young boy who could only stammer spoke clearly. A man whose legs were stiffened and who was unable to kneel could bend his legs and kneel without pain. Crooked spines were made straight. After we left that town, the pastor called us and reported the revival was continuing. Instead of a lifeless mid-week service, a child whose tongue was tied was healed, and he began to speak plainly. Another lad who had not been able to concentrate on his school work was prayed for and was

125

able to read difficult passages he could not have possibly read before.

God is alive! We wanted Christians and sinners alike to know it. Christians do not need to be powerless, fearful and lifeless. Church services do not need to be boring and dull, with people singing listlessly and actually sleeping during the sermons. Teenagers should not need to turn to the occult world to see power. The awesome presence of the Holy Spirit that filled the church at its birth is still present today, able to give new life and vitality to a nearly dead church that is dragging tiredly through a sin-corrupted world.

How can any of us be content until we see the entire body of Christ awakened with fresh life and vigor and power? Then we would have a living Jesus to offer to a Christ-starved world.

A revival is merely a group of Christians seeking what God wants them to be. The world seeks to offer much to keep this from happening.

Our next meeting would find a congregation setting fire to one of the world's favorite tools—a trap used to ensnare many Christians, to keep them prayerless and powerless.

The blaze would be talked about in many parts of the world.

21

I will set no wicked thing before mine eyes. *(Psalm 101:3)*

Paul was able to preach the Word of God boldly wherever he went. Since he belonged only to God, and did not belong to a church or denomination, he could not be kicked out of one. He could preach without fear of men. He was free to preach against, not only the sins of the world, but also the sins of Christians. He exposed their envy, discord, pride, jealousy, spiritual laziness, love of materialism and pleasures, lack of witnessing and lust—and he called it all sin.

He was either loved or hated wherever he went. Some, who had hidden their sins behind their cloaks of self-righteousness for years, were not happy with him as he exposed their deadly spiritual pride. Others wanted to hear the truth about their spiritual condition, so they could confess and forsake their sins and find a fresh, victorious life in Christ.

One sermon he preached in nearly every church was *"Who Is In Control of Your Mind?"* Most of the congregation would sit up straight when they heard that question, and would think, "I am!"

"But God should be!" Paul would tell them. "The Bible says, *'Let this mind be in you, which was also in Christ Jesus'* (Philippians 2:5).

"The problem is that you want to keep control of your mind. God wants to control it, and the devil is viciously trying to gain control of it. There is a war over your soul. The devil wants it. Jesus died for it. And the battleground—the place where the entire war takes place—is your mind."

"The devil offers you drugs...they destroy minds. He offers Transcendental Meditation...that empties minds so he can fill them. He uses ESP, Ouija boards and other tools of the occult world to open your mind to his powers, so he can ultimately control it. And if the devil once gains control of your mind, he has gained control of you. It is your mind that controls your body. God says, *'As he (a person) thinketh in his heart, so is he'* (Proverbs 23:7)."

"God has given us a list of things we should keep our minds upon. *'Finally, brethren,'* He says, *'whatsoever things are true...honest... just...pure...lovely...of good report...if there be any virtue, and if there be any praise, think on these things'* (Philippians 4:8)."

"This is a *commandment*, not a suggestion, to the children of God. You would not have to take sedatives, sleeping pills and fill psychiatric offices, if you just heeded God's counsel, *'Thou wilt keep him in perfect peace, whose mind is stayed on thee'* (Isaiah 26:3)."

"God says we should bring 'into captivity every thought to the obedience of Christ' (II Corinthians 10:5)."

"He warns, 'to be carnally minded is death; but to be spiritually minded is life and peace. Because the carnal mind is enmity against God: for it is not subject to the law of God, neither indeed can be' (Romans 8:6-7)."

Christians would nod and say, "Amen! Fine sermon! Young people shouldn't get involved with drugs, ESP, TM and the occult world. What is this generation coming to anyway?"

But Paul's next sentence would abruptly silence all the amens and stop all the nodding of heads.

"Can you watch television night after night, day after day, and obey God's commandment to think on true, honest, just, pure, lovely things while you are filling your mind with rape, murder, fornication, adultery and blasphemy? Can you think about things that are of good report while you watch the news of bad report, and become more and more depressed and pessimistic and allow fear to drive out your faith?"

"Many of you don't attend movies in a theater. But you watch the same movies in your home, either through videos or television programming."

"And what a waste of the precious time God has given you to labor in His harvest field. What would the disciples have accomplished, after Jesus returned to heaven, if they had spent their time watching television and sipping cokes? Can you imagine Jesus himself sitting, absorbed in television, rather than saying as He did at just twelve years of age, *'I must be about my Father's business?'*"

"Wasted hours—wasted days—wasted years—a wasted life."

"You have replaced the family prayer and Bible reading that used to be part of every Christian home with hour after hour of television viewing. You bring your child to Sunday School once a week for one hour, and wonder why he strays away from the church and the

129

Lord as a teenager. He has had thirty hours a week of school in an environment that forbids God and His Word and another thirty hours in front of the glamorous, sin-filled world of television. God commands, *'Fathers, provoke not your children to wrath: but bring them up in the nurture (training) and admonition (counsel) of the Lord'* (Ephesians, 6:4)."

Still no amens. No one nods. But as Paul continues his sermon, some of the younger people begin to nod their approval.

Even before Paul had preached this sermon, he had opened the revival meeting by asking how many members of the congregation would turn off their television sets during the five days of the meetings, and spend the time they normally spent watching TV, praying and inviting friends to the services. By the time he preached this sermon, some Christians could hardly wait for the services to end, so they could settle comfortably again into their former routine of mind-numbing television viewing. The pastors were often the most miserable without their television entertainment.

But there were always some families who would realize that television was actually controlling their lives and their homes, and they would respond by either getting it under control or getting it out of their homes.

"Jesus said," Paul would remind them, *"if your eye, hand, or foot offend you, cut them off. 'It is better for thee to enter into the kingdom of God with one eye, than having two eyes to be cast into hell fire: Where their worm dieth not, and the fire is not quenched"* (Mark 9:47-48).

"The apostle Paul counsels us, *'Dearly beloved, let us cleanse ourselves from all filthiness of the flesh and spirit, perfecting holiness in the fear of God'* (II Corinthians 7:1)."

He preached this message on a Saturday evening in a Battle Creek church. The church had had as many as twenty-seven hundred people in Sunday School. Sunday evening, folks began to arrive at church for the final service. Many brought their television sets along and threw them in a pile in the church parking lot.

Paul was praying for the last few people who had been part of a line of sick people that had reached all the way around the church and back into the foyer. Many of the people had left. I was at the organ when I heard some strange popping noises. I slipped off the bench and opened the side door of the church. There was a huge blaze, and televisions were exploding with a muffled pop. Someone had poured gasoline on the pile of TVs and they made a huge bonfire. The assistant pastor was there, talking to some people. We learned later they were reporters. The local paper had the fire blazing on their front page the next morning.

By the end of the next week, the *Associated Press* of the United States, Japan, Germany and Canada had picked up the story. Paul Harvey had carried it further on his daily newscast. Some of the articles in the press were unbelievable. I was ready to stay home forever. Paul went to our printer's office and passed the barbershop as he walked down the street. "There he is," men were saying, pointing at him. "That's the one. He's out going from city to city, burning TVs." Paul went into the barbershop. "Where are my matches?" he said, going

131

through his pockets. "I see you have a TV in here." They laughed nervously, and he left.

"You are going to have to buy the groceries from now on," I said, while he told me about it. "I am staying home. People think we are crazy! Did you read the article from our home town? It says, 'The protest burning was organized by Evangelist Paul Wilde, who spoke at the church last week on the evils of television."

"As if all we are trying to do is to set fire to people's television sets!"

"And look at this headline in a Detroit paper. '*An Evangelist Speaks and TVs Bite the Dust*.' Then it goes on to describe you as a saxophone playing evangelist who brought his wife, a 1974 Dodge van and vocal chords to the Battle Creek area to address a fundamentalist church. It says the thirty-three year old preacher has a style that is fiery. Isn't that awful?"

The paper did quote Philippians 4:8 at the end of the article though, so I guess something good came out of it. It's not every day a Detroit newspaper quotes an entire Bible verse.

The Grand Rapids daily paper reprinted most of Paul's sermon and mentioned how we had gotten rid of our TV in disgust six years earlier. The Hart paper printed a front page, truthful article about what had happened. At least two papers reported what really happened and why. Other reporters just couldn't resist labeling Paul as a fire-breathing evangelist.

My seclusion in the house that week wasn't too peaceful. The telephone rang constantly. The majority of the calls were from radio and television stations across the country. A radio station that claimed an audience of 250,000 listeners called during a talk show program and asked Paul what kind of sermon prompted people to burn their television sets.

"Do you really want to know?" Paul asked him.

"That's what I called for!"

Paul preached the sermon for the next twenty minutes over the telephone and over the air waves. Apparently it upset some people because afterwards the talk show host let people call the station to ask "*Rev. Wild*" questions. (During the TV burning, everybody automatically dropped the "e" off our name and addressed Paul as Rev. Wild.) There were a few young people who heartily shouted amen to his sermon. The older people were irate. It made us realize that the addiction of older people to television is one reason our churches are dying. Elderly prayer warriors are what holds the church and its pastor up before God for His blessing and anointing. Now they were engrossed in soap operas and murder stories.

A question on a popular television game show was, "Who was the preacher who burned the TVs?" "Rev. Wild," the contestant answered and got the point.

What hectic days those were. Paul appeared on two television talk shows, *Haney's People* on WKYZ and the *Lou Gordon Show* on WKBD. He used every opportunity during those interviews to present the Bible verses he had used in his sermon, and we prayed the Word would wake up some Christians who were slumbering spiritually in front of their TV sets, while an entire world waits to be harvested for Christ.

It did wake some up. We received letters from all over the United States. One Catholic man from

Plymouth, Michigan wrote and commended the church for its stand against sin. A mother of seven from Colorado said their TV had broken twelve years earlier, and they had enjoyed their family life so much during its absence that they had never had it repaired. A lady wrote from El Monte, California commending the "fearless stand" of the church members.

A father in Sun Valley, California wrote to say their TV was gone and they were going to allow Jesus Christ to take control of their home.

A woman from Evansville, Tennessee just wrote to say, "Praise God! All His people are not dead, nor asleep!"

A Nazarene adult Sunday school teacher from Little Rock, Arkansas wrote to say that when she dared to mention the evils of TV, she really faced opposition from her class.

A couple from Hamburg, New Jersey wrote, "After living outside of the United States for twenty years, we have retired to our home in New Jersey and have been shocked and saddened to discover that television, which used to be a marvelous educational and entertainment medium, has become a corrupting vice—indeed, a poison that has already affected people's thinking to the extent that they see no wrong in the ever increasing profanity."

I wonder what that couple thinks today. If you have a TV you really don't notice its subtle changes too much. But we see one only once in a few weeks or months. And every time we see it, it is worse. There are very few 'bleeps' now, as a bad word is cut out. They are just allowed to roll from any person's foul mouth.

We received a beautiful letter from a family who turned their television set off every single evening to spend sixty to eighty minutes reading the Bible and praying with their children.

One of our most inspiring letters was from a Wisconsin couple who had thrown their television set away and began using their extra time for the Lord. They became houseparents in the *Penal Christian Home for Boys*, leading delinquent boys to Christ.

A man ended his letter with, "People will probably laugh at you and ridicule you for being so radical about righteousness."

He was right!

The *Associated Press* quoted the General Secretary of the Church of the Nazarene as saying the burning was an irrational act.

Some of our forthcoming meetings were canceled by pastors who were worried that Paul would arrive at their church with a Bible in one hand and a torch in the other.

But we kept going to churches that kept their doors open, and to others who agreed with Paul's stand and opened their doors to us.

It helped us, during the uproar caused by the television burning, to read in the Bible about the uproar in the city of Ephesus after Christians there had thrown their false gods into a raging bonfire. They too had become "radical about righteousness"!

The office of the *National Enquirer* called us from Florida. They said they wanted to write an article about

Paul and our family for their weekly publication. They interviewed Paul over the telephone. Later they called and said they were flying a photographer to Michigan to take a picture of our family. When he contacted us from the Chicago airport to set up a time to take pictures, Paul said, "Read me the article you have written first." He didn't quite trust the *National Enquirer!*

Their article did not in any way uplift Jesus Christ and righteousness. It merely discussed the changes in our home after we got rid of our TV. Paul told him to forget the picture and the article, feeling it was a waste of time. After about three more calls, he gave up.

I was relieved. I hate having my picture taken. And I definitely didn't want them taking a picture of our kids!

All eight of them had the mumps!

22

Commit thy way unto the Lord trust also in him; and he shall bring it to pass. (Psalm 37:5)

One of the reasons we had so reluctantly begun our faith venture of working for God full time was our bills. In the years we had worked for Him, God had always taken care of our family's daily needs, but we never were left with an abundance to pay our past bills.

One afternoon in the castle, I was praying about the bills we still had and God gave me a beautiful answer to my prayer.

I saw the bills, pictured as I always visualized them, as a huge, insurmountable mountain. This time, the mountain was directly in front of us, and Paul and I were briskly walking hand in hand straight for it. "We will hit it!" I remember thinking. "We have to stop walking."

The Lord said, *Keep walking*, and we kept walking at our brisk pace. The mountain loomed menacingly right ahead of us. We just kept walking. The farther we walked, the smaller the mountain became, until finally it was so small, we just stepped over it.

I was given such a peace about our bills that day. For the first time they lost their menacing hold on me. For the first time I *knew* they could not destroy us or keep us from walking for the Lord. And for the first time I realized that one day we would just step over them, and they would all be paid. Somehow, God would provide us with enough money to pay them. Until that day, we would just keep walking for our wonderful Lord.

One morning Paul received a telephone call from Dallas, Texas. A brother in Christ said, "Paul, there is an evangelist I want you to work with. I want you and Carolyn to do his music for him. Name your price! We will pay you whatever you ask for."

"Who is he?" Paul asked.

"This man is unbelievable!" was the answer. "He is fantastic! You will love Him! You have heard of men laying hands on people and they fall over...slain in the Spirit? Well, this brother doesn't even touch them. He just blows on them, and over they go! Why, just last night, over one hundred people fell over. One hundred people! Can you believe it?"

"Hold it!" Paul interrupted. "How many were saved? I don't care how many got blown over! How many sinners found Jesus? How many backsliders returned to Christ?"

"Paul," the caller continued, as if he hadn't heard Paul's question, "you can't refuse! This is an opportunity you won't get again! I am telling you—name your price, just to travel and do his music."

"No," Paul answered. "I am not interested. I don't have a price. I belong to God, and I am not for sale. I don't like the idea of a bunch of people being blown on and falling over. I am more interested in seeing people on their knees repenting."

"Paul, now listen! Don't judge this man and his services. Go see for yourself! He will be in Detroit next week. Just do me a favor by going and listening to him. Call me back collect, and we will make arrangements for you to travel with him. Introduce yourself to him in Detroit. He will be looking for you. You will love him."

"All right. I will go to Detroit," Paul finally consented.

The next week, we drove to Detroit where this man was holding services. We arrived about forty-five minutes early, and went into the huge church. Paul went to the restroom, and I was in the vestibule waiting for him to return. We were alone in the church, except for one man. He was walking towards me to shake my hand, when the Lord warned me, *Don't let this man shake your hand.* I was startled by such a command, and I smiled and said hello to the man and quickly walked to the other side of the vestibule.

He again walked towards me with his hand extended, and again God impressed me with the same warning. I dodged his hand the second time. This happened three times before Paul returned. By the time Paul arrived, there were others entering the church, and we sat down.

We endured the song service. People got caught up in the beat of the music and began swaying and dancing in a sensuous, worldly way. I think we would rather have been in the midst of one of the world's dances than in that church that night. At least the world's vulgar motions are not done in the precious name of the Lord. Finally the speaker was introduced. I was shocked! He was the man I had dodged!

"Before I begin tonight's message," he said, "I want to tell you about my special message I will be preaching tomorrow evening."

"I urge every one of you to come. I am going to reveal a great secret to you! I am going to tell you how to impart the power that is within you to everyone you meet ...just by bodily contact. You can impart your power by just brushing someone's shoulder on a street, by shaking someone's hand..."

By shaking someone's hand? This man who wanted us to sing for him could transfer his power to another person by shaking their hand? Oh, was I relieved I hadn't let him shake my hand!

As Christians, we cannot impart Jesus, the power that is within us, to someone else by touching them! If we could, we would touch the whole world, beginning with our relatives! All we can do is tell people about Jesus— then they must go to the Father, the same way we did, to receive Christ as their Savior and Lord. The people that touched the hem of Jesus' garment during the days He walked this earth were instantly healed by His power. But they came to Him to touch Him to receive their miracle! He did not walk the roads of His day, touching people and transferring His power to them, without them even being aware of what He was doing!

We didn't want this man shaking our hands, brushing our shoulders or blowing on us. The world itself would not be price enough to sing one song for him.

"Name your price!" What a trick of Satan's! The Bible says, *"Ye are bought with a price: (Ye were not redeemed with corruptible things, as silver and gold...But with the precious blood of Christ. Therefore glorify God in your body, and in your spirit, which are God's"* (I Peter 1: 18-19, I Corinthians 6:20).

We returned to Hart and continued laboring for God. Someone else could sing while this evangelist blew!

We heated the castle with fuel oil. It had a six thousand gallon, underground tank to feed the huge furnace that heated the monstrous building. Everything went along fine the first Michigan winter, and we stayed toasty warm without much problem. Then the Arabs raised their oil prices to the United States, and the price of fuel rose steadily. In the past when we had only small homes to heat, sometimes we would run out of fuel oil, and Paul would go to a gas station with his five gallon can and pour it in our tank to keep us warm until the delivery truck arrived to fill it.

But can you imagine pouring five gallons of fuel oil into a six-thousand gallon tank? It would be a mere drop. And can you imagine keeping those oil-guzzling furnaces running? We kept the temperature in the castle about 68 degrees and the offices about 60 degrees, and it still cost us about $350 every nine days to only partially heat our building. Somehow the money was always there for us to pay the oil company when their truck arrived, but what a waste of the Lord's money. It was going up in smoke!

We didn't know what to do, so we went to our heavenly Father for advice. We felt His leading to sell the castle. We began to wonder if we had done wrong to buy it. We were not going to be using it for retreats again. We didn't know what to use it for. Why had we bought it in the first place? We decided to put it up for sale.

We talked to the ones who had freely given their time to help us fix the place up. Every one of them favored selling it because of the expense to heat it. After we advertised it for sale, we had countless potential buyers who were considering purchasing it for a children's home or a home for the elderly. They all would leave, seemingly enthusiastic about buying it, promising to call us later. They would check with the regional office about its possibilities as a licensed home and immediately they would lose interest in the building.

We would contact them later. "We have decided not to buy it," they would invariably say. "The office at Grand Rapids says the building is condemned and could never be licensed for a home."

We finally called the regional office ourselves. "Have you seen our building?" Paul asked. "It is completely restored. It is beautiful. It is true it had been condemned as a convalescent home for the county, but it has never been condemned for anything else. Would you please stop falsely informing our potential buyers?"

They assured him they would.

The following week we had another potential buyer, who said he was definitely going to buy the castle. Then he called Grand Rapids.

"Oh, no, we can't license that building as an adult foster care home," he was told. "It is condemned."

We went to the Lord again. "Now what?" we asked. His answer was to obtain the license ourselves and then to sell it.

We called the state offices and in just a few weeks we had our "condemned, impossible" building fully licensed as an adult foster care home. We opened it up to receive residents who could no longer live alone and needed someone to cook and care for them.

Our first guest was a frail, elderly lady, brought to us by her children. Paul talked to her for five minutes and then fled to the part of the castle that was our home. "Carolyn, I can't enter that poor lady," he said. "She's so pitiful. You will have to talk to her."

I went to talk with her, and the forlorn lady, nearly eighty years old, moaned, "Oh, I wish my mama was here with me. She would take me home and take care of me. She would help me now." Accepting those elderly people into our home and lives was a heart-rending experience, but we were glad we were there to help them. Too often their children made extravagant offers to visit their parents faithfully every weekend, and we would never see them again.

In a few weeks, we had nine extra guests in our home. We were still traveling in revival meetings, and we had hired a registered nurse to care for our guests.

While we were in New Mexico, we called home and discovered our nurse would be quitting the day we arrived home. We were scheduled to be in Wisconsin the following week. We knew we could not continue to travel and run a family, a paper, and a home for the elderly too. We not only had a family of eight children, but three full-time jobs. It was impossible to keep up with all the work. Something had to go!

The devil immediately tempted us to quit traveling from church to church and just stay home and care for our family and the elderly.

"Pure religion and undefiled before God and the Father is this," he quoted from the Bible, *"to visit the*

fatherless and widows in their affliction, and to keep himself unspotted from the world" (James 1:27).

Then he added another line: "It would get you completely out of debt too. You could become millionaires!"

We battled over our decision for a few days. We knew after a few days of talking to our Lord that our responsibility in the body of Christ was to win souls. However rewarding and good it is to take care of the elderly (and we did enjoy it), this was not what God had called us to do.

This time when we advertised our castle for sale, the state employees who licensed homes could not discourage our potential buyers! We had a fully licensed home with nine residents in it!

We listed it with a realtor. It didn't sell right away. The furnace kept thirstily guzzling expensive fuel oil.

Finally one evening, Paul and I were desperate. "Lord," we prayed, "this home is robbing us of our time. We can't travel with this additional responsibility. We will just give this whole place away, if somebody will just take over the home and our payments. Then we can better serve you."

Obviously, that was what the Lord was waiting to hear. We would once again walk away from our possessions and any potential profit, in order to serve Him better. The very next morning, our realtor arrived, handing us an offer on the castle for $120,000. We accepted it in a hurry!

How we praised God! As soon as we chose Him, rather than money, He blessed us with a financial profit!

We had only $36,000 altogether in our castle, and we sold it for $120,000.

For the first year since we had organized *Michigan for Christ*, we were able to take our annual $15,000 salary, and we paid most of our bills with it. Our mountain of bills was just a molehill now. Soon we really would step over it!

We believe God led us to an abandoned "Castle" to provide money to pay our bills and to further test our desire to put Him and His work first in all that we did.

23

*O Lord, I know that the way of man is not in himself;
it is not in man that walketh to direct his steps.*
(Jeremiah 10:23)

We were driving home from a revival meeting one day, when Paul asked me, "Carolyn, do you feel a real peace in your heart about our work for God?"

"No."

"Neither do I. I can't understand it. We are seeing countless souls saved. Churches are being revived. What is wrong? I don't feel happy inside."

As Paul was questioning our ministry, the Lord spoke to him, *Go back to where you got off.*

Got off? Had we gone contrary to God's will? It just happened that we were driving through Muskegon at that moment, and God reminded Paul of the commandment He had given him three years earlier to start a church in Muskegon.

This time we had no people to talk us out of it. No people? How could we start a church with no people? Paul knew he would have no peace of mind until he yielded to God's call to Muskegon—people or no people!

A couple of days later, Paul and I attended a revival meeting in Muskegon. A black evangelist from California was preaching. Brother Colburt's message that evening seemed just for us. "Why aren't you doing what God told you to do?" he asked in his powerful sermon. "You know God has given you a command. You know you have not obeyed Him. Are you afraid? Don't you know that if God tells you to jump through a brick wall, it is up to you to jump and it is up to God to provide the hole? I'm warning you. God is warning you. He's told you once. Now He is telling you again what He has called you to do. And this time, you had better obey Him. Many people will be saved if you obey God's call. If you don't, things are going to get worse and worse for you."

"This is terrible," Paul whispered to me and to Brother Bacon, another dynamic evangelist and friend we had come with. "This whole message is aimed straight at me. He's even looking straight at me! And did you notice his finger? It keeps pointing right at me! This is awful!"

It was settled. We were on our way to start a church in Muskegon—people or no people. We drove past the little brick church to see if it was still available. It wasn't! There was a service being held in it that very night.

The following Sunday evening we were scheduled to hold a concert in a nearby Reformed church. Paul asked his realtor friend who was a member of the church if he knew of any available church buildings in Muskegon.

"I believe there may be one available," he answered. "Two of our churches there are considering a merger."

He gave Paul a name to call for further information. Paul was told there could be a future merger and there might be an available church.

Nobody seemed to know when or even if the merger would take place, so Paul asked the Lord what to do. The answer came swiftly. *You move to Muskegon. I will provide a church.*

As Brother Colburt has said about the brick wall, "You jump—then, and not until then, God will provide a hole." God was again leading us to walk in faith. When we moved, He would then provide a building.

We moved our family to Muskegon. It was a difficult move for all of us. We had many dear friends in Hart, and we hated to leave our brothers and sisters in the Lord. We didn't want to leave the friendly printers who had faithfully helped us get our paper out every month and had been so good to work with. We didn't want to leave a town of friendly business people. Kathy hated leaving all her friends.

But we moved. In December, we were in our new home. In January, we received a call that the merger was taking place and we were invited to discuss the purchase of a church building with the church boards of the two merging churches. On February 1, we bought the church.

We did not have money to buy it, even though we had made a considerable profit on the castle. We had sold the castle on a land contract. We had traded the land contract for a brand-new colonial duplex. We didn't believe our buyers would make their payments without pressure, and as a preacher, Paul knew he couldn't pressure them every month for money. When God told us to move to Muskegon, we traded the duplex for a mini-ranch close to Muskegon. Until these houses were sold, we would not have any money.

So we went to the board meeting with no money to buy the church. We handed the presiding officer of the meeting three typewritten offers and asked them to make their choice. They chose our offer to buy their church and parsonage, with a down payment of $10,000 to be paid one year from the date of purchase.

We went home from the meeting in a daze. "What have we done?" we asked ourselves. "Are we crazy?"

We had just bought a church and its parsonage. We had agreed to make payments of $426 a month and to pay $10,000 at the end of one year. Now that wouldn't be so bad, except for one thing...our church had no congregation! All we had was an empty church, eight children, Paul and myself! Oh, yes...and payments!

Then came the next big step in our faith walk, and for Paul, it was one of the hardest. The following morning he told me, "Well, I can't put it off any longer. I have to do it today."

"Oh, no," I groaned. "Are you sure?"

He was sure. He went to his desk and called all the pastors of the churches where he had revival meetings booked. He canceled every single one of them, and when he had finished every call, he had canceled our entire source of potential income. Once again, we looked to God alone as our source.

We advertised on the Muskegon radio stations and in the newspaper, "Revival Meeting! Hear Evangelist Paul Wilde at the New Testament Church of Muskegon." (We discovered later the name of our church was a poor choice. The rumor circulated that we didn't believe in the Old Testament, even though Paul often preached from it and we even published an Old Testament Bible course. We had named it a New Testament church because we, as Christians, are under God's New Testament, or New Covenant.)

The evening of our first meeting, we arrived early. "Will anyone come?" we wondered anxiously. We placed our two sons at the door as ushers, and we kept glancing hopefully at the entrance. Finally someone walked in. Never was anyone more warmly welcomed! There were actually people coming! About thirty people came that first evening, and by the end of the week, Paul was preaching to over one hundred people. He announced the revival meeting would continue for another week. By the second week, we heard people commenting to one another, "I didn't even realize this church was here," or, "Where is the pastor of this church?"

That week Paul announced that he was the pastor and God had called him off the road to start a church. He announced the opening church services would be on the following Sunday.

On Sunday morning, nearly fifty people came. Paul taught the adult Sunday School class, and I taught everyone else, from two to eighteen years old!

We put every ounce of strength we had into the church. We made mistakes. It was quite a transition for Paul to go from a hellfire-and-brimstone evangelist to a compassionate shepherd of a flock! But coming down the aisles during just about every single service were countless sinners accepting Christ, in spite of our mistakes. Many families were saved. Numerous young people, disillusioned after coming through the turbulent sixties, found Christ was the only answer to life. Young couples, their marriages floundering, were reunited at the altar where they gave Christ control of their lives and homes.

We opened our church every Tuesday from one o'clock in the afternoon to ten o'clock, for what we called *"Spiritual Clinic."* Many troubled and burdened people came to Paul's study, and we counseled and prayed with them together.

Many couples of all ages who had miserable home lives came to talk to us about their troubled marriages. Paul would ask the husband to relate the problems of the marriage as he saw it. Then the wife would do the same. Paul and I would listen to their complaints, but more importantly, they listened to each other. For the first time, they heard their partner's viewpoints and feelings. Communication had invariably broken down years before, because any attempt at constructive criticism had developed into a heated war of slinging stinging insults at one another. In Paul's office, they would control their anger, because a preacher and his wife were listening to them. They would finally hear and understand the other's real complaints. By the time each had listened to the other, their problems were usually solved. We went through Scriptures with them, giving them God's order for their home.

We could help them understand the Scriptures, because we had experienced many storms in the early years of our own marriage. It wasn't until we went to the founder of marriage for His advice, that we found

He had a divine order for every home—I Corinthians 11:3. There is a chain of command that stretches from God to a child:

1. God, the Father
2. Jesus, His Son
3. Man
4. Woman
5. Child

The vicious sin of rebellion destroys homes. Children rebel against their parents and destroy a peaceful home. A wife rebels against her husband's authority, and a marriage is wrecked. Man rebels against God, and an entire family is bickering aimlessly through life. Thank God that Jesus had no rebellion. He said to His Father, *"Not my will, but thine, be done"* (Luke 22:42).

We could also advise the defeated, backslidden Christian, because we had been there too. Prayer and the reading of God's Word keep our relationship with God alive and full of love and joy. Just as a husband and wife need open communication in order to have a good relationship, every Christian needs open communication with God in order to have a good relationship. We talk to Him through prayer. He talks to us through His Word.

God had shown us the importance of prayer in our own lives in several ways.

When Paul was first being called into the ministry, Janet, only four weeks old, became deathly ill with pneumonia.

One morning, I knew for sure she would die. She could hardly breathe.

I prayed, "O God, please heal her. Save her life, Father."

I received an immediate answer from God. His answer was, *When you and your husband kneel down together and pray for Janet, I will heal her.*

Pray together? That was the last answer I wanted to hear! We had begun our marriage by praying together. Then one evening after we had prayed, Paul said, "It seems senseless for both of us to pray. We both say about the same things.

"Well," I interrupted in a huff. "Don't worry about it being senseless! I won't *ever* pray with *you* again!"

Some ending to a prayer meeting. God used Janet's sickness to change that rebellious decision to never pray with my husband again. It took just the rest of the day nearly seven years later, watching and listening to Janet's labored breathing, to melt that bitter grudge down. The second Paul arrived, I met him with, "Janet is worse. Will you pray with me for her? I am sure God will touch her if we pray together."

We prayed together. God touched Janet while we were still on our knees before Him. Her fever instantly broke, and she breathed freely. God had used our precious baby to further prepare us for His service. How could we have possibly served Him by ministering to others, when we couldn't even pray together because of my stubborn vow during a feud? We have had many wonderful prayer meetings together since that day—in our home, in Paul's study, in empty churches, and in motel rooms across the country.

One day a few years later, we had the privilege of being at a dinner table with Mrs. Beall, the founder of a church that began as a Sunday Bible class for neighborhood children in the city of Detroit, and now has about five thousand members. She looked at Paul and me, just young in the ministry.

"Children," she said, "I have just one word of advice for you. Pray. Pray. If you pray, things will go right for you. If you neglect prayer, everything will go wrong."

Often discouraged Christians came in to *Spiritual Clinic*, looking miserable and defeated.

"I just don't feel close to God any more," they would begin tiredly. "My church...my pastor...my husband... my wife....

After they had finished blaming their backslidden condition on someone else, we would ask them, "When did you quit reading the Bible? When did you stop praying?"

We had learned many years before that a Christian who has open, daily communication with God is a victorious, undefeated Christian. Praying Christians seldom need counseling.

One Sunday morning, we looked over our congregation. Paul and I were the oldest people in our church— at thirty-four years of age!

"We will have to pray in some older people!" we said after the service. "We need mature Christians to help all these new ones."

154

We didn't have anyone but brand-new Christians to teach the Sunday school classes or to help with the youth. God answered our prayer with a beautiful Christian couple. Everyone who met Brother and Sister Jolliff loved them. We put him right to work teaching our adult Sunday school class and leading our testimony services. He was in his sixties, but had as much enthusiasm and pep as our younger people.

The only problem we had with him was that every fall, as the temperature began to drop and the leaves fell off the trees and storm doors and snow tires were put on, Brother and Sister Jolliff headed for Florida. So every winter we lost our adult Sunday school teacher. We were always happy to see spring arrive, not only for reasons everyone loves to see spring arrive, but also because we knew that when the snow was all melted we would see Brother and Sister Jolliff come bounding back into church, praising the Lord.

The spring of 1978, we all welcomed them back. He spent one Sunday with us, teaching Sunday school and leading the testimony service. The following morning, Brother Jolliff left us again, this time for a vacation that will last an eternity, in a place where there is no snow, no pain, no parting, no death. We're all looking forward to seeing him again.

Meanwhile, God had sent us another precious elderly saint. Brother McCastle always had a vibrant, up-to-date testimony for his Lord. He passed on to his heavenly home too, but many of us still remember the advice he gave our church full of newly saved Christians. He told them, "There are two times to testify. One—when you feel like it. Two—when you don't!"

Simple wisdom, but those words came back many times to many new believers, not only when they were in church during a testimony meeting, but also when they were among lost sinners who needed to hear about Jesus.

God answered our prayer for older people in yet another way. The young couples began praying that God would save their parents. It was something to hear their prayers at the altar and remember back to what they had been just months before. They had been the heart-break of their parents, often wandering aimlessly through life on drugs. Now they were praying that God would save their parents' souls!

God answered their prayers. Many parents came to see what had caused their son or daughter to begin living a holy, clean life, and they found that Jesus was also the answer to their unsatisfying quest for material gain.

Steve always prayed the longest and the hardest. He had caused much grief for his parents. They often wondered if he was alive or dead as he wandered from one end of the United States to the other on drugs, hitch-hiking aimlessly. He had been in the Navy, but had gone AWOL so many times he had finally been dis-charged. One desperate, but successful attempt to escape authority found Steve going hand over hand from one docked ship to another, dangling from an electrical cable thirty feet above the ocean.

He had wandered into a bowling alley in Muskegon, and had been handed a tract at the door. He read it and asked the young man who had given it to him for further information about the gospel. The young man

156

directed him to our church. The following morning, Steve came and found Jesus Christ at the altar. His search for peace of mind, happiness and something to live for was over. He had found Jesus.

Steve's parents were not prepared to take too much preaching from Steve after the way he had lived his life. But Steve kept praying, and even though his preaching wasn't effective, his prayers were.

His mother was on the verge of a nervous breakdown because of a crumbling marriage. After she signed herself into the hospital, Steve's dad, a very successful businessman, came to church and was saved. What a conversion he had, as he met Jesus Christ face to face, while Steve knelt beside him with his arm around him, praying, weeping, and praising God all at the same time.

When he left church that evening and went to the hospital to visit his wife, she noticed a difference in his face the second she saw him. "He was all lit up," she said later. "All his burdens were gone. I could see it just by looking at him."

Now Steve had his dad join with him as he prayed for mom. Mom was saved the following Sunday. After her meeting with Jesus, she was no longer threatened by a nervous breakdown. The Prince of Peace had entered her life. God healed their marriage and gave them a joy they would not have believed possible on earth, until they had experienced it for themselves.

God not only answered Steve's prayers for the salvation of his parents. Other parents were saved too.

Paul and the newly saved young men went throughout the area, inviting people to church and to Jesus Christ. Slowly our church filled up with people.

When we saw people giving their lives unreservedly to Christ and finding peace and happiness for the first time, we were glad we had finally obeyed God's call to start a church in Muskegon. He was filling our empty church with precious souls.

Our monthly payments were always made on time, and money was coming in for our $10,000 down payment. We lived about sixteen miles from our church. It was the closest house we could find where the owner was willing to trade us his house for ours. It was a nice home in an absolutely perfect setting. It had twelve and a half beautiful, wooded acres, a pond, a creek, two barns, horse trails, and much to Kathy's delight, even a horse had come with it. It was a dream place for raising our eight children.

When we moved into it, I said to Paul, "I don't know how long God will let us live here, but even if it is just for a few months, I really appreciate it."

We all appreciated it. Our only problem was that we had to drive in to our church usually once and often twice a day, and we could not be with our children as much as we needed to be.

We decided to sell it and move closer to the church, not only to spend more time together as a family, but also to be more available to the people God had given Paul to pastor.

We sold our beautiful mini-ranch after living in it just one year. We received money from its sale just two days before our $10,000 payment was due on our church! We have discovered again and again in our faith walk that God always provides. To test our faith, He also nearly always waits until the last possible minute.

158

We found a home large enough for our family in Muskegon. We moved from our beautiful place in the country, knowing we would never live in a place that could even compare to it until we arrived in heaven.

We would discover two years later that Jesus gave us a promise that cannot be broken. He said, *"There is no man that hath left house...or lands, for my sake, and the gospel's, but he shall receive an hundredfold now in this time, houses...and lands, with persecutions; and in the world to come eternal life"* (Mark 10:29-30).

24

All scripture is given by inspiration of God, and is profitable for doctrine, for reproof, for correction, for instruction in righteousness: that the man of God may be perfect, thoroughly furnished unto all good works.
(II Timothy 3:16-17)

When God had told Paul to pastor a church in Muskegon, Paul had looked forward to it like a person looks forward to going to a dentist. He did not want to be a pastor! But while Paul pastored, God constantly saved souls. All the peace and happiness we had lacked had now been restored, because we *knew* we were where God wanted us to be, doing what He wanted us to do.

We were able to reap an additional benefit while Paul pastored, a benefit we hadn't had while he was traveling from church to church holding revival meetings. We were not only able to bring someone to Jesus Christ, but now we could watch as God changed the newborn soul into His image. We watched people literally become new creatures in the Lord. We saw God change a drug pusher into a preacher, a drug user into our bass guitar player, a hardened sinner into our smiling usher, a successful businessman into a faithful servant of God, a broken young man into our drummer, and a wandering hippie into our adult men's Sunday school teacher.

Every week we saw God miraculously mold useless, wasted lives into His servants. Whether a man was rich or poor, held a high position or no position in this world, God could change him into a beautiful person.

Many of the people in our congregation had no knowledge whatsoever of the Bible. Others had very limited knowledge of God's Word. One afternoon, Paul was pondering Jesus' parable of the sower who sowed the seed—the Word of God. Some seeds fell by the wayside, where they were stepped upon and eaten by birds. Some seeds fell on a rock, and sprang up, then withered away, because they lacked moisture. Some seeds fell among thorns, and were choked by the thorns. Some seeds fell on good ground and bore fruit plentifully. (See Luke 8:5-15)

God spoke to Paul as he pondered these Scriptures. *You are responsible for the type of ground these seeds are falling upon.*

Paul knew he was faithfully preaching the Word of God, seeds were being sown, and they were bringing a harvest of souls. But was he providing a place where Christians could grow until they themselves were bearing fruit? The Bible held the answer to their growth. Paul read, *"As newborn babes, desire the sincere milk of the word, that ye may grow thereby"* (I Peter 2:2).

Paul thought about the sheep God had made him responsible for and their various backgrounds. As new Christians, they needed to feed upon the Word of God, so they could grow into mature servants of God.

He prayerfully put together a ten-week course, and enrolled the people in the new *Bible Foundation class*. Nearly our entire congregation signed up for the course.

The first week was all about the blood sacrifice from the book of Genesis to the death of Jesus, the final blood atonement for our sins. Christians who had been faithful church attenders throughout their entire lives were amazed at the truths in the Bible they had never been taught concerning the blood.

The second week they learned what the Bible says about water baptism, from the Old Testament washing of the sacrifice in the Tabernacle to the New Testament baptism of Jesus and His command to be baptized.

The Sunday afternoon following the second class, we met those who wanted to be baptized at the swimming pool we had rented at the YFCA. Those of us who had been previously baptized sang songs of praise to our Redeemer as the new believers were baptized.

Steve was among the group that was being baptized, and his sister had come to watch him. I looked at Lynn. I noticed she had the only unhappy face among us. I knew she could be saved. I went over and stood by her, hoping and praying for an opportunity to tell her about Jesus. No opening seemed to come.

I went over to Paul just as the last person was being baptized. "Could you give an altar call or something?" I asked him. "I believe Steve's sister will get saved, if you just give her the opportunity."

Paul was always ready to see another soul saved. He would fish for men wherever and whenever he got the opportunity.

He said to the nearly seventy people in the room, "Before I dismiss this baptism service, I want to tell you about something that happened right here not too long ago. We brought a group down from Hart to be baptized. A middle-aged woman was among them. Her husband came to watch her be baptized. God impressed me to give an altar call that afternoon. Curly, her husband, knelt down on this cement, and gave his life to Christ. Curly (everyone called him Curly because he was bald) was baptized immediately after he was saved. Curly was not an old man, but just a few months later he died suddenly of a heart attack, and I was speaking at his funeral. I am glad I saw Curly repent and find a Savior before he left this world and began eternity in the next."

"What about you?" Paul continued. "Have you come to watch someone be baptized this afternoon? Are you saved yourself? You don't know how long it will be before you are ushered into eternity. Are you ready to meet Christ?"

Lynn responded to that altar call by kneeling on the cement, finding her Savior, and being baptized immediately afterward. She is a new person today—she has found happiness along with the rest of God's people!

The third week of the Bible class was a teaching on the baptism of the Holy Spirit, again beginning with the Old Testament sacrifice being consumed by fire and going right through to the New Testament.

By now, older Christians discovered they had not even learned many of the basic truths of God's Word. They became excited as they began to really study the book that had been placed on their coffee tables and neglected. Old and new Christians began to grow in Christ.

The fourth week invariably began with husbands and wives arriving with their shoulders squared and their minds set. But as Paul began teaching on *God's Order for the Home* God changed hardened hearts through His Word. Families left that class determined to put into practice in their homes the rules and commands given by God. God healed marriages and mended many broken relationships between family members as they began to follow His commandments for a happy home.

Paul continued the course with *God's Order for the Church Conditions to Inherit God's Blessings.* (People were amazed to learn that night that every promise in the Bible has a condition with it.) *Basic Christian Living* was the next class followed by *Bible Prophecy I and II, Soul Winning* and *Altar Call Work.*

Oh, how the Word of God began to stabilize Christians! They were no longer tossed about by every wind of doctrine, but began to grow as they lived by biblical principles. When Paul finished one ten week course, he started right over, teaching another class of newly saved Christians. Every ten weeks, we would have a new class of people who had been saved during the previous ten weeks.

We also stressed the importance of a daily home Bible study. Some Christians literally devoured the Word at every opportunity. Others scarcely read the Bible, depending on us to feed them. We wanted everyone to feed daily on the Word. We searched for a Bible course that would help them get into the Bible—from Genesis to Revelation. We knew the Holy Spirit would teach them, if they just would read it!

All we could find were teaching courses that skipped from book to book. So we printed a course ourselves, beginning with Genesis 1. Many of the people began taking it. They would read a chapter, then answer questions on that particular chapter. When an Old Testament truth related to a New Testament teaching, they were instructed to read the New Testament reference. Many were thrilled to be able to understand the way the Old Testament and the New Testament relate to one another so beautifully. The course also forced people to slow down and dig out of the chapter answers that they otherwise would have skimmed right over. Because of the Word, the new Christians and older ones, who had never grown up in Christ, began to grow and bring forth fruit.

We were excited to see some of the men decide to go to the rescue mission once a week on their own. By teaching and enthusing others, we were not just laboring in the harvest field ourselves, but we were seeing others begin to roll up their shirt sleeves and begin to labor in the fields that were white unto harvest!

We set one evening aside each week as *"Laymen's Night."* The men of our church, young and old, preached the Word of God and shared its ageless truths with others. We found we could all learn from even the newest believers.

These same new Christians continued to dedicate their Saturday mornings to going out into the streets and homes to witness to people.

The teenagers got together Friday evenings and passed out tracts and witnessed to people on the streets and in the mall.

Paul made arrangements with a Muskegon radio station to have a weekly broadcast. He took new Christians with him, and many people were stirred as they listened to their testimonies.

God not only gave us a harvest of souls, but He continued to heal the sick, as Paul reached out in faith and prayed for them.

During one prayer meeting on a Wednesday evening, we watched as God performed a miracle on a young boy's feet. Johnny had been born with club feet that not only turned in but were different sizes. As Paul prayed for him, God touched Johnny's feet, and we watched in amazement as his feet straightened. His feet became completely normal before our eyes. Johnny was so excited. He had been wearing either a cast or braces on his feet and ankles since birth. The one desire of his heart was to wear tennis shoes like other boys. As soon as church was dismissed, his parents took him straight to a shoe store and bought him his first pair of tennis shoes!

One Sunday evening during a testimony and song service, a Catholic woman ran to the altar and replaced her faith in religion with personal faith in Jesus Christ.

Her daughter, Connie, was one of the young Christians who had been praying for the salvation of their parents. Connie and her husband, Chon, had knelt at the altar in our church, making their peace with God. They had partially owned and managed a home for former mental patients who were trying to make the transition from the institution to a normal life.

Chon had been on the verge of a nervous breakdown himself. One evening at the altar he wept and prayed, pouring his burden out to the Lord. We prayed with him, but he couldn't seem to find peace. Chon couldn't cope with caring for and living with the people in his licensed home. He and Connie had married, and had begun their married life living in the home as resident managers. He was condemning himself, because he just could not take the pressure of caring for these people. We showed him from the Bible that there is a body of Christ, with different members who fill different positions. "Not everyone can do everything," we told Chon. "Don't try to be something you are not called by God to be. If God had called you to work with these people, your nerves would not be shattered right now."

Chon found peace that evening by realizing he was not failing God because he couldn't take care of these people. He and Connie sold their large home and moved into an apartment. Chon became a new person, happy again, at peace with himself and with God. He not only became our drummer, but is now a faithful prayer warrior in the body of Christ.

God was answering the prayers of Connie and Chon. Connie's mother poured her heart out to God at the altar. For forty minutes she knelt, repenting and thanking and praising the Lord for saving her. Paul knelt beside her and heard her saying in her Spanish accent, with tears streaming down her face, "I love you, Jesus. I love you, Jesus."

She finally got up and sat on the front seat. Paul led the congregation in a few worship songs and prepared to dismiss the service. She turned to me in amazement. "Isn't he going to preach?" she asked. Then she noticed the clock. "I thought I prayed for about five minutes!" she exclaimed. "I have been praying for forty minutes?" She couldn't believe it.

A short time later, she died of heart failure in her home. She had been a politically active woman and had friends in every phase of Michigan government and many in Washington, D.C. But we thanked God that just before her death, Jane had personally met the only friend who would count in eternity—Jesus Christ.

25

No good thing will he withhold from them that walk uprightly. O Lord of hosts, blessed is the man that trusteth in thee. (Psalm 84:11-12)

Our church ran smoothly during the fall, winter, and spring. But when summer came, so did vacations. Some churches in Muskegon closed their Sunday school programs and their evening services in the summer, because teachers and students would be on vacation. We kept ours going, but there were always at least one teacher and several students missing. We were happy that the people were able to take vacations, and get away from their daily routines for much needed rest. But it was hard to have at least a quarter of our congregation missing each week!

Paul said more than once, "If we had a place—a campground or something where people could spend their vacations, then we would grow instead of losing half our people during the summers."

One day after he had made that comment, our song leader, a car salesman, said, "I know where there is a campground not too far from here. It might be for sale."

"Is there a "For Sale" sign out in front?" Paul asked.

"No, but I have never seen it being used when I have driven by. Drive out and look at it," Dave suggested.

The next time Paul saw Dave, Dave asked, "Have you checked on that camp?"

"No," Paul answered. "I am sure that if it was for sale, there would be a sign out in front."

Another few weeks passed. Dave asked Paul again, "Have you driven out and looked at the camp yet?"

"No. I will. I will."

One evening, Dave and Pat came to our house. "Have you looked at that camp yet?" came the inevitable question.

"No," Paul answered. "Let's go look at it right now, together."

We drove about seven miles out of the city of Muskegon. There we found the most beautiful camp-ground we had ever seen. We couldn't believe it was there, just outside the city God had called us to. Nestled among the beautiful oak trees were eight nice houses, a long dormitory, a huge lodge, a beautiful cafeteria, and other small buildings. We drove along a hill and looked down to a beautiful lake. The camp looked vacant. Could it possibly be for sale? One of the houses had a light on inside. Paul knocked on the door and was almost afraid to ask, "Is this camp for sale?"

"Yes, it is," came the reply.

Paul came bounding back to the car. "It is for sale!" He told me. Right then, we knew that somehow this place was ours. How God was going to work out the finances for us to buy it, we didn't know. We just knew from experience that He could, and He would!

Paul received further information from the caretaker of the camp. The campground consisted of one hundred forty acres, about a quarter of a mile of lake frontage, all the buildings, the eight houses we had seen, and two cottages on the lake besides. We were told it had been given originally to Billy Graham, who had turned it over to *Youth for Christ*. The *Youth for Christ* director had made it into *Youth Haven*, a place for delinquent boys, and then had sold it to *Child Evangelism Fellowship*. *Child Evangelism* had used it as a training center for several years, and then had moved to Warrenton, Missouri, leaving the campground unoccupied for two years. We knew that night that somehow, someway, God was going to make *Michigan for Christ* its next owner.

Paul called *Child Evangelism Fellowship* the next day and learned we could purchase the camp for $230,000. Two hundred thirty thousand dollars! We didn't even have $1,000! But we had a God who had brought us this far by faith, and somehow would take us into that campground. We felt it was our "promised land" that He was leading us to, and He was telling us to go against all obstacles and possess it. It was ours.

We sent Child Evangelism a $500 deposit, asking them to hold the camp for us until we could work out our financing. Now all we had to do was to obtain the remaining $229,500!

Our congregation was excited with us about the camp. Many of them lived closer to the camp than they did to our church.

We went to the bank. One bank officer said, "We can loan you the money in the spring. Come back then." In order to raise our down payment, we would have to sell the property we still had from the sale of the castle. Our payments would be huge, but we would receive rental payments from the houses at the camp. There were six single family houses, three duplexes, and one three-family unit. That meant we would receive rental income from fifteen families!

Then one night Paul couldn't sleep. He prayed, and God asked him, *Did I call you to be a full time landlord?*

Paul knew the answer. God had called him to be a full time preacher and soul winner. Paul and I drove out to the camp the next morning. We got out of our car and walked through the beautiful grounds and around the beautiful buildings. We went down to the lake, and walked hand in hand along the beach. We could feel God's presence. We knew God did not want Paul to become a full time landlord. We also knew the camp was ours. It was where we were supposed to be.

God suddenly gave us the idea to sell the houses, with the lots, to people in our church. Questions came in quick succession. Would we all get along, even though the houses were some distance from one another? What if someone decided to sell his house and sold it to sinners? What if parents died and left their house to ungodly children? How could we maintain it as a Christian camp if we sold the houses? Immediately an answer came. We could sell someone a house and lot with an agreement that if they ever sold their house, we would have a ninety day option to buy it back at its appraised value. If a house owner died, we could have a ninety day option to buy the house and pay the appraised value of the house into his estate. Then we could sell the house to another Christian family.

Everyone would be happy and best of all, it would be maintained as a Christian campground.

We felt a peace about all those houses now. We could sell them. They would not be our responsibility, robbing us of time we could be spending for the Lord.

Then one day we heard some shocking news. A Muskegon businessman was telling people he had made arrangements with *Child Evangelism* to purchase their camp. We called Missouri. "Yes, we have received a $10,000 deposit from this individual," they answered.

All we have from you is $500. If you are still interested, send us an agreement to buy it with a substantial deposit right away and we will refuse this man's offer. We would rather sell the camp to a Christian organization." (None of us knew it at the time, but there had been a stipulation when the camp was first donated that it could never be sold to anything but a fundamental Christian organization.)

All we knew was that we needed money to hold the camp. We knew the camp was ours, but *Child Evangelism* didn't know it yet! We had to convince them we were their buyers, even though they had only $500 from us and $10,000 from another party. We surely didn't have $10,000 to give them!

We went to a realtor and listed our house for sale. He brought the entire staff of realtors, through our house one morning, and included in their party was the owner of the company. Paul introduced himself to him and told him a little about the camp we were going to buy.

The realtor said, "Paul, if I can help you in any way, let me know." Then he added, "If you need a loan or anything, I will help you."

His offer continued to ring through our minds. We went to his office a few days later. "Could we borrow some money until our house sells?" Paul asked.

"Yes," our new friend answered. "How much?"

Paul hated to tell him. "Twenty thousand dollars," he answered.

Later that week, we received a personal check from Barth for $20,000. We didn't have to pay it back to him until our house sold.

We mailed it to *Child Evangelism Fellowship*, with an agreement to buy their campground. The agreement stated that if we failed to purchase the camp, we would lose the entire $20,000! Another big step of faith, but we knew God would somehow provide the remaining $210,000! We just didn't have any idea how!

On July 10, 1978, we bought the camp. The same day, three couples from our congregation purchased five houses. Their purchase gave us our down payment and we financed the rest. We still had four houses in the camp to sell and one beautiful, large, nearly new house to live in ourselves.

Before that day at the bank, we had had many seemingly insurmountable obstacles. At one point, our lawyer had said, "What you want to do is impossible! You don't have the money to buy the camp. Right?"

"Right," Paul nodded.

"You have to sell houses in the camp in order to buy the camp. Right?"

"Right!" Paul agreed.

"Then how are you going to sell what you don't own? You can't buy until you sell! And you can't sell until you buy! There is only one answer!"

"What?" Paul asked eagerly.

"Get yourself another lawyer!"

"Bill, you can do it, if anybody can," Paul said. "There has to be a way."

Bill consented to go talk to the Vice President of the bank. Between them, they came up with a way to work it all out.

Then there had been other obstacles. For example, one of the original stipulations on the property was that if liquor was ever sold or consumed on the property, the entire campground could revert back to the woman who gave the property or to her heirs. We certainly didn't intend to sell or consume liquor on the campground. But if someone had wandered on the beach from the public road and consumed liquor before we got them off, we could lose the camp and all our money. No bank would lend money on property with such a stipulation.

Our county surveyor discovered a later document that took the word consumed off the stipulation. He hurdled one problem after another for us, meeting with our lawyer to discuss the latest hurdles. We discovered that we could buy all of the campground except the two cottages and part of the woods until a life lease was terminated, so the price of the camp was reduced to $175,000 with an option to buy the rest later for $55,000. God used the surveyor, the Vice President of the bank, and our lawyer to iron out many such difficulties, until the final day when we were able to purchase the campground.

Actually, the day we bought the camp and our three buyers bought their houses, none of us had any money.

The couple who purchased three houses had money coming in later that week from the sale of their house. They hadn't closed the sale by July 10, so they borrowed their down payment from the bank. They also borrowed enough to loan our second buyer money until he sold his house. The third buyer borrowed money from us (which we didn't have, but we would receive that day from the sale of the five houses we didn't own) until they could sell their house. We hadn't yet sold our house. So we all went into the bank that day, and not one of us had any money to buy a thing. But one couple bought three houses, two couples each bought one house, and we bought an entire campground! No wonder our lawyer became frustrated! Only the Lord could have worked all that out! We were left with a mortgage of $70,000!

We drove out to our camp after a full day of signing papers at the bank. As we drove through the camp roads, a peace came over us. We knew we were exactly where the Lord wanted us to be. He had led us here. As before, we didn't know how long the Lord would leave us here, but our faith in a good future was having Him for our Guide and Provider.

We walked through the campground and its buildings. There were a tennis court and playground area for the children. It was the only Michigan camp we had seen that had fully winterized buildings. And they were beautiful. There wasn't an auditorium big enough for our

176

church, but as soon as we sold the church we had, we planned to build a big tabernacle on the grounds. The dormitory was fantastic, with twenty private rooms, two apartments, restrooms and two nice lounges. We had a beautiful, nearly new home, large enough to comfortably house our family of ten. There was the large cafeteria that would seat over one hundred people. It had a fully equipped kitchen and a huge fireplace. The ceiling of the cafeteria had been woven in Taiwan and shipped here. The lodge was an especially nice building overlooking the lake. It included an auditorium with a fireplace and enough room to seat about seventy five people, rooms we could use as a library, Sunday school classrooms, a nursery, and a wing of more-than-adequate offices.

We had acres and acres of beautiful woods, with trails winding through them. A path led to the lake and the beautiful beach area. We could already visualize the picnic tables and swinging benches we would have under the maple trees, where people could sit and view God's beautiful sunsets. It was a beautiful lake. Paul had always loved the water, but we had not gone to the public beaches because of the semi-nudity of sunbathers.

Here our children could swim in a Christian atmosphere. Our children—how they would love it here! How good God was to us! We had forsaken houses and lands to follow Him. And He blessed us with an entire campground, full of houses and beautiful land!

We had followed Christ even when it meant leaving our children, our hearts often aching, when we had to go to another revival meeting. Now He had put us here as a family, where our church and our offices would be just steps from our home.

The children had been moved often, away from their schools and friends, and they had not complained about their frequent separations from us. Now God had blessed them with a place where any child would love to live.

All we could say was, "Praise God, from whom all blessings flow...and flow...and overflow!"

26

Let your conversation be without covetousness; and be content with such things as ye have: for he hath said, I will never leave thee, nor forsake thee. So that we may boldly say, The Lord is my helper, and I will not fear what man shall do unto me. (Hebrews 13:5-6)

We sold our church building and houses in Muskegon, and moved into the countryside surrounding the city. What a peaceful place to live. Our realtor friend who had loaned us money came out from the pressure filled city, and walking through the camp, remarked, "This place is therapy." Our neighbors are all Christians. Our children have Christian friends to play with.

How God has blessed us. We often think back to the time Paul was fighting God's call for his life. Eleven years ago, we didn't know God was the loving God that He is. We had read about His concern over the sparrow, that small creature of His vast creation. We had discovered through our own experiences, as we walked by faith, holding to God's hand, that He truly does love us enough to guide us, protect us, provide for us and care for us.

David once asked God, *"What is man, that thou art mindful of him?"* (Psalm 8:4).

We have wondered, "Who are we, that God guides us so lovingly through this life?"

We know the answer to that question. We are nothing. God is everything. We are just one family who has put our trust in God. And He has not, and will not, and cannot, ever let us down.

Oh, we have had the rough times, the trials. We watched the tabernacle that we had built in the campground crumble. Its collapse was the result of a severe, nine-day snowstorm and faulty workmanship. It was a geodesic dome, designed to seat four hundred people. On January 7, 1979, at eleven o'clock at night, we watched in horror as it fell to the ground and lay in a broken heap of rubble. It was about two weeks from being completed. We had already paid the builder $37,700, which we have still not recovered.

That was a trial, but we did not fall with the building. God has blessed us abundantly with material blessings, but we have learned the truth of Jesus' words, *"A man's life consisteth not in the abundance of the things which he possesseth"* (Luke 12:15).

When spring arrived, we cleaned up the mess of the broken building and by faith signed a contract with a different builder for another tabernacle.

Were we discouraged? Yes. Did we question the fall of our building? Yes, we did! Trials are not fun! Everyone on this earth—including the Christian—has troubles, trials, failures, discouragements, and heart-aches, but the Christian has something the world does not possess. We have our God. We can just grip His hand a little tighter during our troubled times, and someday, a little further down the path of life, we will look back and say with assurance, *"We know that all things work together for good to them that love God, to them who are the called according to his purpose"* (Romans 8:28).

The second tabernacle, a larger one than the first, went up by faith. We ordered pews, by faith. We invited our friend, Brother Leonard Ravenhill, author of *Why Revival Tarries*, to speak in our first services.

We invited him, by faith, trusting God that our building would be finished by September 21, 1979. Our opening day reminded us of that opening day in our castle a few years earlier. That time our church was ready, but our guest rooms were not ready until the last minute. This time our dormitory was ready for those who had made reservations for the special meetings—but our church wasn't ready—until the last minute!

The opening day was one of the most hectic of our lives. There had been a delay when the builders could not find the right light fixtures to place in the already installed sockets. The pews had not yet arrived from California. The builders were frantically scurrying around, trying to finish the building. The telephone company was having difficulty wiring us into the local gospel radio station, as they had asked to carry the meetings live on the air. The painters were still there with their scaffolding.

Paul and I, all our "camp family," and even my mother who had come to attend the meetings, were cleaning around the workers as they continued to make one mess after another.

At three o'clock that afternoon, the last light fixture was hung. Lights! We all rejoiced when we saw that they actually worked! The workers left about six o'clock. Some men from the church arrived with folding chairs from the high school. (Since the superintendent of the schools lives in our camp, he helped us obtain several hundred chairs until our pews arrived two days later.) The painter was just finishing painting the exterior doors when people began to arrive. The vacuum cleaners were put hurriedly away, and we changed from our work clothes and rushed back to the church. The church was beautiful. It was finished—at the last minute, as usual—but it was done just in time for its first guests.

God is still blessing us with beautiful services. People are continually being healed. People are continually being saved.

One precious Christian who attends another church has slipped out to ours on two different occasions for prayer. God has instantly removed two different tumors as she has reached up to Him in faith for His healing touch.

One morning a few months ago, I heard an elderly woman behind me whisper to her husband towards the end of Paul's sermon, "Oh, I have a terrible pain in my side." Just after the service was dismissed, she slumped unconscious on the pew. Several of us went to her to pray. Steve felt for her pulse, and found it beating weakly. Then it stopped. Her life slipped into eternity even as Paul and others continued to pray for her. She was gone. Paul began to go to the telephone to report her death, when he felt impressed by the Lord to pray just one more time. He asked that the others join him as he prayed once more, this time for her to come back from death. Suddenly while he was praying, Mrs. Fessenden, who is in her seventies, leaped to her feet, praising and glorifying God. One second she was laying prone on the pew, the next instant she was on her feet crying exuberantly, "Oh, He is right here! Jesus! Can't you see Him! It's Jesus!" She was looking upon her Savior and Healer, and no one there doubted it, even though our eyes were not open to what she was seeing.

Just a few weeks earlier, this same woman had been instantly healed of cancer. Her doctors verified her healing, and the major surgery she had been scheduled for was canceled.

As great as these miracles are, we praise God that He is still touching people with even greater healings—the healing of sin-sick souls.

Since our arrival in Muskegon, God has sent to us the unchurched—the people who are down and out and ready to give up their search for peace and happiness in this life. We are reminded of the words Jesus spoke when He was asked why He ate with publicans and sinners: *"They that be whole need not a physician, but they that are sick... I am not come to call the righteous, but sinners to repentance"* (Matthew 9:12-13).

There had been Dave and Pat, who had just been led to Christ by a friend before we had arrived, and were not yet in a church. They attended nearly every one of our services faithfully, drinking in the Word. Dave had been a drug pusher, but now he is a preacher in our organization. He and Pat went to the town of Coopersville, found an empty church, and went door-to-door to every house in the town, inviting everyone to their new church. They are faithfully serving God there.

There was Ron, who found the Lord in his living room while watching the *700 Club*. After he repented, he called the number given for further counsel. The counselor directed him to our church, and God has changed his whole life. As our faithful usher, he can say with David, "I had rather be a doorkeeper in the house of my God, than to dwell in the tents of wickedness" (Psalm 84:10).

There were Mike and Sharon, saved out of a ruined life of misery, fear, drugs and sin. Mike had worked in a factory with Dick, who is our song leader now. He had one day asked Dick how he could keep smiling while working over hot molds in temperatures that were sometimes over 100 degrees. Dick told him the Lord was his joy, and Mike and Sharon attended church and found that joy themselves.

There was Dan, disillusioned from the teachings of college, a member of the campus Communistic movement, who replaced his faith in Communism with a faith in the coming King of kings, Jesus Christ.

There are Mark and Jacci, a young couple whose lives were nearly ruined by Mark's alcohol and drugs, but who found Jesus as their Savior and Lord just a short time after moving from Chicago into a duplex in our camp. They are on fire for Jesus now, going out door-to-door to tell people about their new Savior.

There are Del and Becky. Del, a former rodeo performer, was saved; Becky had returned to Christ after a life of wandering from Him. Now they have been out in their own neighborhood, witnessing for the Lord.

Whole families have found Christ. Louie had been embittered against Christians and mocked his wife,

Gloria, when she attended church. Louie is now "one of those Christians" himself, and since he found Christ, his four children have found Him too.

There is Ethel, who had been saved in a meeting held by the Palermo Brothers, but did not find a church home until we opened our church doors. She is the type of Christian who would argue that she isn't worth much. All she does is open up her arms and home to every needy child in her neighborhood. She feeds them, gives them birthday parties with her limited funds, comforts them, tells them about Jesus—and just plain loves them.

There is Ellen, a girl who had denied Jesus to become a Moslem, the religion of her fiance. Since there was no mosque in her area, she had found an apparently unsaved or backslidden preacher, who not only agreed to marry them, but agreed not to mention the name of Jesus Christ during the marriage ceremony or in his prayers. She had moved to Pakistan with her new husband, but became disillusioned with life there and returned home. What a joy it was to see her kneel at the altar of our church, ask for forgiveness for denying Christ, denounce the false religion she had embraced, and receive the Lord into her heart and life.

These are just a few of the literally hundreds of people who have found Christ, or a closer walk with Him, after we bought—by faith—that empty church in Muskegon.

There is no greater happiness on earth than working in the Lord's harvest field. We can honestly say we love it. Oh, there is persecution, but that is part of the Christian's life. God gives us the grace to keep going

185

on in spite of persecution and lies, and to keep walking and working for Him.

Satan's most treasured possessions are the souls of men. Nearly everyone has a prized possession that they allow no one else to touch. Our Elizabeth has a faded baby quilt that she dragged along with her every place when she was a toddler. She still takes it to bed with her, and woe to the one who dares touch it!

The prize possessions of the devil are the souls of men. We Christians can touch *anything* in Satan's kingdom, but when we lead souls out of his kingdom into the kingdom of his enemy and our King, Jesus Christ, we had better prepare ourselves for battle.

When Paul first began winning souls to Jesus, the war was on. Jesus described the devil as the father of lies who has no truth in him. One of his chief weapons is a lie, and he uses it often against us.

When we called our church the *New Testament Church* he said we didn't believe in the Old Testament. When the first issue of *Sound of the Watchman's Trumpet* came out (we dropped "Watchman's" after our first few issues) he linked it to the Watchtower and called us Jehovah's Witnesses. When we moved to the campground, he wagged his head and said, "Must be another Jonestown." When we lead teenagers to Christ, he labels us *Moonies*.

Oh, he gets angry! He will use anyone he can to spread his lies. At first, when we were new at this spiritual warfare, we made a serious mistake. We began to defend ourselves by refuting his lies. One day we realized not as many souls were being won to the Lord in our ministry. We were spending all our time on defense instead of offense! The only reason the devil creates his lies is to stop the Christian warrior! The best way to defeat him is to keep right on taking souls from his kingdom and persuading them to kneel before Jesus and serve Him as King!

Jesus never took time to defend himself. He was accused of being a glutton, winebibber and blasphemer, but He ignored the lies and went on to redeem a world of dying sinners to himself and a heavenly inheritance.

At one point in our faith walk, Paul set his eyes on the devil, his lies, and the people the devil used to spread the lies, and felt himself and his witness being crushed by them. "O God, help me!" he cried out, and God led him to open his Bible. He opened it to this passage, *"Then spake the Lord to Paul in the night by a vision, Be not afraid, but speak, and hold not thy peace: For I am with thee, and no man shall set on thee to hurt thee: for I have much people in this city"* (Acts 18:9-10).

What a God we serve! He saw Paul near defeat, and lifted him up by His assurance that He was with him. And if God is for us, who can be against us?

Our enemy is most pleased when he can stir up a friend or loved one against us, for he knows that this will hurt us the most, and he will stoop to anything to keep us from leading his captive souls to Jesus.

David went through that torment, and he was ready to retire from being the King of Israel to become a hermit because of it! He said:

> *My heart is sore pained within me: and the terrors of death are fallen upon me. Fearfulness and trembling are come upon me, and horror hath overwhelmed me. And I said, "Oh, that I*

187

*had wings like a dove! for then would I fly away,
and be at rest. Lo, then would I wander far off,
and remain in the wilderness.*

*For it was not an enemy that reproached me;
then I could have borne it: neither was it he that
hated me that did magnify himself against me;
then I would have hid myself from him: But it
was thou, a man mine equal, my guide, and mine
acquaintance. We took sweet counsel together,
and walked into the house of God in company*
(Psalm 55:4-7,12-14).

Not too long ago, I was deeply hurt by loved ones. I
decided to become a hermit right in my own house.
First, I decided I would never talk to people again. The
devil has a way of turning and twisting our words as
Christians and then using them against us. So I would
just quit talking! If I was forced to be among people, I
determined I would listen, smile, frown, nod or shake
my head. Beyond the words *hello* and *good-bye* (good-
bye being my favorite) I was through with talking. I
decided to arrive at church before anyone else and go to
my office and pray until just before church began. Then
I could go quickly to the organ. After church was
dismissed, I could play the organ until everyone left.

Well, I actually did all this for a few weeks. Fear of
people did this to me. Because a few people turned
against us, I was convinced everybody would.

Then one night I awoke out of a sound sleep and the
Lord was urging me to open His Word. I opened the
Bible and Jesus' words spoken on the mountain to a

multitude of people two thousand years ago came down

through the ages to me, *"But I say unto you, That ye resist not evil: but whosoever shall smite thee on thy right cheek, turn to him the other also"* (Matthew 5:39).

I started to read on, but instead read that verse over and over until Jesus' message in those words began to fill my whole being: *When you are hurt by someone, don't run and hide from people. Get right back in among the people and make yourself vulnerable to be hurt again.*

Those words of Jesus turned my life around that night. I realized the devil had accomplished exactly what he had wanted to accomplish by his lies. I had retreated in fear to my own little world and had quit tampering with his prized possessions—the souls of men, women, teens, boys, and girls.

I had always thought that verse was just referring to a physical slap on the cheek, and since I had never been slapped, I didn't think it applied to me. Now I realized its deeper meaning: When you are hurt, don't run and hide from the people God has called you to minister to. Get right back into the battle and make yourself vulnerable to be hurt again—and again—and again.

All the persecution in the world cannot even be measured against the blessing of leading just one soul to our Savior. Just last evening, we had a blessing we had never had before. We received a telephone call from Mark, who had just rented a house in our camp. He told us a new Christian was at his house talking to him, and asked if we would come and join them. We knew why the new Christian was there. He was trying to lead his first souls to the Lord. He had prepared the way for us, by telling Mark and his new German bride about Jesus Christ and what He meant to him. Mark and his wife, who had just arrived in Muskegon from Germany to join her husband, knelt and received Christ into their lives and hearts that evening. Roni prayed to God in her German language. We could understand a few of her words as she wept and prayed—forgive, sins, come, heart. Hearing her pray the sinner's prayer in German was a new experience for us. It was beautiful. We all praised God that the only house the young man could find to rent for himself and his new bride was right in our campground.

We are not just winning souls ourselves anymore—that is only part of our work. We now have a congregation of dedicated Christians who are going out regularly to win souls in our area. They have a map, and are crossing out one street after another, as they go out in rain, shine, sleet or snow to harvest people for our Lord's Kingdom. Last week, we had the privilege of seeing our three oldest children, all teenagers, join the group.

Sometimes people will say, as they come to their doors, "Are you a Jehovah's Witness?" What a tragedy that most Christians leave the harvest of a lost and dying world to a false cult!

We've come this far by faith. We do not have to pray for a loaf of bread or a dozen eggs any more. We now trust God for the greater needs of the ministry. If we ever do get in the position again where we are praying for our next meal, we know now that we have a God who will provide it for us.

After working for God alone for the past eleven years, we can say as the apostle Paul said nearly two thousand years ago, *"I have learned, in whatsoever state*

I am, therewith to be content. I know both how to be abased, and I know how to abound: every where and in all things I am instructed both to be full and to be hungry, both to abound and to suffer need" (Philippians 4:11-12).

If we lost all our earthly possessions tomorrow, we would continue our faith walk with God. We would be content. You see, our contentment does not come from our material blessings, though we praise God for all He has given us. Our contentment comes from the deep abiding peace that comes from knowing we have a Father who loves us and cares for us and guides us through life. We don't know what our future holds. It is enough to know God will lead us through it, one faith step at a time. God himself is our contentment.

"For this God is our God for ever and ever: he will be our guide even unto death" (Psalm 48:14).

Where do we go from here? We will go wherever and however our Guide leads us. We believe great things will happen in our camp, as people come from far and near to be saved, healed, and brought closer to God. We have heard the comment several times, "I felt the presence of the Lord just driving into your camp." This one thing we know:

We've come this far by faith,
Leaning on the Lord.
Trusting in His Holy Word,
He's never failed us yet.[1]

Addendum

And now it's ten years later, and we're in Foley, Alabama.

This is the part that is so hard to write about. What happened in that beautiful land of peace and tranquility that God provided?

What happened in the Garden of Eden?

Another time... another place... but the same old serpent of destruction and lies was at work.

After being in the beautiful campgrounds for five years and working in the Hart and Muskegon area for over fourteen years, seeing countless souls saved, families healed, and backsliders restored, the serpent struck with all his venomous poison.

I don't feel free to go into all the ugly details, because people we still love and are praying for were involved. The devil filled hearts with hatred and mouths with lies. We stood on the Word of God, and took a stand against sin. We were ridiculed for that stand. We heard, "This is a new day! You're old-fashioned! Preaching against adultery and fornication will no longer be accepted in our society!" And one man vowed to destroy us because of that stand. Men of God have faced it before and will face it until Jesus comes. Our lives were threatened and in danger. Our girls were no longer safe. We answered our telephone day and night to obscene filth or just breathing. People were contacted, lied to, and warned not to come to our church. One woman coming to a revival meeting had to drive off the road to keep from being hit by another car that was purposely driving toward her head-on. We learned the meaning of the Psalmist's words, "They have sharpened their tongues like a serpent; adders' poison is under their lips."

We were crushed and exhausted, and yet we kept on, because that is what God's people are supposed to do. We had always kept going during adversity, and by God's grace and strength, we always will. We prayed a lot, wept a lot, and pleaded with God to intervene and stop it all. But the hatred just intensified. The people God had given us to shepherd held us up in prayer and love support, but even that wasn't enough. We were literally burning out from battle fatigue, and getting nowhere. Every time a new family would attend our church or a lost soul was saved, they were contacted and lied to. Our ministry was no longer effective.

Then God did speak to us—but not in the way we expected. Every time we opened our Bibles to feed on God's Word and for His instruction, we would read some startling passages—passages that we had read before, but now seemed to be ignited by the fire of God, that burned their way into our hearts.

Passages about Jesus...

And behold, the whole city came out to meet Jesus: and when they saw him, they besought him that he would depart out of their coasts. And he entered into a ship, and passed over.
(Matthew 8:34-9:1)

*Then the Pharisees went out, and held a
council against him, how they might destroy
him. But when Jesus knew it, he withdrew
himself from thence.* (Matthew 12:14-15)

*The Pharisees went forth, and straightway
took counsel with the Herodians against him,
how they might destroy him. But Jesus withdrew himself with his disciples to the sea...*
(Mark 3:6-7)

*After these things Jesus walked in Galilee: for
he would not walk in Jewry, because the Jews
sought to kill him.* (John 7:1)

*Then took they up stones to cast at him: but
Jesus hid himself and went out of the temple,
going, through the midst of them, and so
passed by.* (John 8:59)

*Then from that day forth they took counsel
together for to put him to death. Jesus therefore walked no more openly among the Jews;
but went thence unto a country near to the
wilderness, into a city called Ephraim, and
there continued with his disciples.*
(John 11:53-54)

And we read passages about the apostle Paul...

*Saul increased... in strength, and confounded
the Jews which dwelt at Damascus, proving
that this is very Christ. And after that
many days were fulfilled, the Jews took
counsel to kill him: but their laying await*

194

*was known of Saul. And they watched the
gates day and night to kill him. Then
the disciples took him by night, and let him
down by the wall in a basket. (Acts 9:22-25)*

*The Jews stirred up the devout and honourable
women, and the chief men of the city, and
raised persecution against Paul and Barnabas,
and expelled them out of the coasts. But they
shook off the dust of their feet against them,
and came unto Iconium. (Acts 13:50-51)*

*When there was an assault made both of the
Gentiles, and also of the Jews with their
rulers, to use (Paul and Barnabas) despiteful-
ly, and to stone them. They were ware of it and
fled unto Lystra and Derbe, cities of Lycaonia,
and unto the region that lieth round about:
and there they preached the gospel. (Acts 14:5-7)*

*There came thither certain Jews from Antioch
and Iconium, who persuaded the people, and,
having stoned Paul, drew him out of the city,
supposing he had been dead. Howbeit, as the
disciples stood round about him, he rose up,
and came into the city: and the next day he
departed with Barnabas to Derbe.
(Acts 14:19-20)*

*And (the magistrates of the city) came and
besought (Paul and Silas), and brought them
out, and desired them to depart out of the city.
And they went out of the prison, and entered in
the house of Lydia: and when they had seen
the brethren, they comforted them, and
departed. (Acts 16:39-40)*

195

The Jews which believed not, moved with envy, took unto them certain lewd fellows of the baser sort, and gathered a company, and set all the city on an uproar, and assaulted the house of Jason and sought to bring (Paul and Silas) out to the people. And when they found them not, they drew Jason and certain brethren unto the rulers of the city, crying, These that have turned the world upside down are come hither also: whom Jason hath received and these all do contrary to the decrees of Caesar, saying that there is another king, one Jesus. And they troubled the people and the rulers of the city, when they heard these things. And when they had taken security of Jason, and of the other, they let them go. And the brethren immediately sent away Paul and Silas by night unto Berea. (Acts 17:5-10)

And when Silas and Timotheus were come from Macedonia, Paul was pressed in the spirit, and testified to the Jews that Jesus was Christ. And when they opposed themselves and blasphemed, he shook his raiment, and said unto them, Your blood be upon your own heads; I am clean: from henceforth I will go unto the Gentiles. And he departed thence....
(Acts 18:5-7)

The list of verses about Paul fleeing cities could go on. After the riot in Asia that had a whole city in an uproar, Paul told his friends good-bye and left for Macedonia.

And then there was David...
David fled from King Saul many times. Once when Saul was threatening to kill him,

Michal, David's wife and Saul's daughter,
helped him escape by letting him down
through a window. He later fled for his life
from his own son, Absalom. How David
must have hurt. Those who wanted him killed
were his own son and his father-in-law.

We knew, like David, that the hurt is deeper when
family members are involved.

Then there is Elijah, the daring prophet of God...

Elijah boldly stood before his king and
declared there would not be another drop of
dew or rain until he spoke the word. "And the
word of the Lord came unto him, saying, Get
thee hence, and turn thee eastward, and hide
thyself by the brook Cherith!" (1 Kings 17:1-3)

There was a man sent with a message from God...

Elisha commanded one of the children of the
prophets to take the box of oil and go and
anoint Jehu to be king over Israel. And when
he had fulfilled his mission, Elisha said,
"Then open the door, and flee, and tarry not."
(II Kings 9:1-3)

We read of Joseph and Mary, after the birth of Christ...

The angel of the Lord appeared to Joseph in a
dream after the birth of Jesus, and said,
"Arise, and take the young child and his moth-
er, and flee into Egypt, and be thou there until

*I bring thee word: for Herod will seek the
young child to destroy him." (Matthew 2:12-13)*

We read our Lord's admonition to His disciples before
sending them out...

*But when they persecute you in this city, flee ye
into another! (Matthew 10:23)*

We had so often preached and stood firmly on the
verses that tell us to stand firm when persecution arises,
that we were blinded to the times God's servants fled.
There are countless times that God's people stood
where they were during a time of fierce persecution, and
saw the salvation of the Lord. And there are countless
times when they simply fled. God sent angels to literally drag Lot and his family from Sodom, but He also sent
Jonah right into the midst of the wicked city of Ninevah
to prophesy its judgment. We began to realize that it
was no disgrace to flee from our situation, and that we
would be in good company—Jesus, David, Elijah,
Joseph and Mary, and Paul had all fled cities at the
Spirit's leading. We also began to understand that we
must be led by the Holy Spirit—and God's leading could
be for us to leave Muskegon.

We prayed for deliverance, but things got consistently
worse. Threatenings increased against us and our
daughters. We got no sleep because of the harassing telephone calls. Our people who faithfully came to our
church in spite of the persecution were threatened. We
felt in our hearts that God did want us to leave. One
day Paul simply picked up the telephone, called a few
of his realtor friends and also dialed his good friend,

Erwin, and asked if he would be interested in buying the campgrounds. If a place of this size sold, it would obviously be God leading us to leave, and we wouldn't argue with God. Erwin's answer was "yes."

We talked to our church people. They didn't want us to leave, but could see no other answer, and all were in favor of the sale. We all could see a tragedy ahead, unless God chose to intervene. It's so hard to even look back and remember this time in our lives. How do things like this begin and spread? Our answer, as always, was in the Word of God. Jesus said, *"(The devil) was a murderer from the beginning, and abode not in the truth, because there is no truth in him. When he speaketh a lie, he speaketh of his own: for he is a liar, and the father of it. The thief cometh not, but for to steal, and to kill, and to destroy"* (John 8:44 and 10:10). John referred to the devil as *Abaddon* in the Hebrew tongue, and *Appollyon* in the Greek tongue. Both words mean **Destroyer**. The serpent had come into our campgrounds and literally destroyed all that we had tried to do. This destroyer despises Jesus Christ. And as long as Christ's ministers are preaching Jesus and seeing souls translated from the kingdom of darkness to the Kingdom of Light, we will be persecuted unto the end. Men of God all face this hatred and these lies during their ministry. And many of them have simply been crushed under the load, and are now out selling cars, selling real estate, and working in offices and factories, their message of salvation stopped, their work for God ended.

During this time, our love for God increased. We felt His divine care and protecting love surround us constantly. We hurt because of what the destroyer was accomplishing, but we knew God had literally sent ministering angels to surround and protect us.

A few days following the telephone call to Paul's friend, we were given a down payment on the campgrounds. The papers were not even signed. Our friend told us the lawyers were working on them, and to let him know where we were in about a month, and he would send them to us for our signature. We took this unusual business proceeding to be a miracle of God, and we realized God was leading us to leave Muskegon.

It was hard to sell the campgrounds. The property was beautiful. We had a beautiful new church. We had two Christian care homes for the elderly. We had built a recording studio to record gospel music. We were ministering to beautiful people whom we had won to the Lord and others whom we had founded in the Word and watched their growth in Christ over the years.

We purchased a motor home to house us and our five girls, and a motor home for an evangelist and his wife who had no home. We stored our belongings. Only our church people knew we were leaving, That night we left our campgrounds, our hopes, our ministry, our dreams. But God didn't leave us.

We had no idea where to go, but God, in His tender mercy and care, had given us a beautiful verse just before we left. We were loaded down with the last minute details of our move, but God kept impressing me to open my Bible. Finally, frustrated because there were so many things to do, just before we left I obeyed God, found my Bible and opened it. I read one verse, and wept. Our primary concern for the past few days was where were we supposed to go. God had given us no direction for our lives. We had labored faithfully in the Hart and Muskegon areas of Michigan for fourteen years. We had been in Muskegon for seven years. Where did God want us—or did He even still want us?

The verse He gave us was Jeremiah 40:4:

> And now, behold, I loose thee this day from the chains which were upon thine hand. If it seem good unto thee to come with me into Babylon, come; and I will look well unto thee: but if it seem ill unto thee to come with me into Babylon, forbear: behold, all the land is before thee: whither it seemeth good and convenient for thee to go, thither go.

Paul and I went over and over those words. I wrote them on a card and we propped them on the windshield of our new motor home. God had set the land before us. Wherever we went, He would look well unto us! What a promise! We feasted on it! We sorrowed as we told our family in Christ good-bye. We loved these people who had stayed by our side and wept and prayed with us through all of our heartaches. It was hard to part from them, and there will always be a special love in our hearts for each one of them. But God had given us a promise. The land was before us. And He would be with us. And His Presence was even now with us, and His glory filled our motor home. His peace surely passes all understanding, and the joy He gives does not depend on the circumstances we find ourselves in! He goes with us when we pass through the fire. However, unlike the three Hebrew children who walked in the fiery furnace with their Lord, we emerged with the stench of smoke on us—the smoke of bitterness against those who professed Christ, but who had hearts filled with hatred, was lodged in our hearts. And there was the resentment against those whom we counted as close friends who simply believed the lies and severed ties with us. We knew a healing would have to come if we could ever be used by our Master Potter again. We started out with more questions than answers. Could God heal us? Would He? Was our ministry done? Where should we go? And what should we do when we get there?

2

Can any hide himself in secret places that I shall not see him? saith the Lord. Do not I fill heaven and earth? saith the Lord. (Jeremiah 23:24)

We traveled two-hundred miles north that night to Petoskey, Michigan, to see our parents. We didn't know when we would see them again, and we spent a few enjoyable days with them.

Then we headed south, leaving just ahead of a raging, December blizzard.

We stayed in campgrounds and attended some good church services held in the parks for campers. While in the Carolinas, we stopped at *Heritage Village* and had a good time camping there.

We parked on the beautiful Daytona Beach of Florida, and the girls played in the ocean, delighting in the warm weather.

Paul and I decided to take the girls on down to Orlando and *Disney World*. They had experienced with us the pressures of our last few months, and we wanted to just have fun with them. We spent a day there, and then headed north, looking at towns and houses along the way. So many of Florida's subdivisions had signs in front of them that read, "No Children Allowed". Since we were still blessed with five beautiful daughters, we just kept traveling. One late afternoon we pulled into *Safari Campgrounds* in Milton, Florida, near Pensacola, to fill up with gasoline.

Paul had decided to go to Arkansas and maybe relocate there. And if we didn't find a spot there, perhaps we would go on to Tulsa, Oklahoma. We had been in contact with Dr. Dudney, who worked in the emergency room of Oral Roberts' hospital. He had ordered and distributed several copies of our books in Tulsa, and appreciated our balanced teaching. At this point in our lives, we appreciated anybody who appreciated us!

The gasoline attendant asked, "Where are you headed?"

"Arkansas."

"Forget it! There is a terrible ice storm, and the major highways have all been closed! Travelers are being warned not to travel unless it is absolutely necessary."

Driving through an ice storm with a forty foot motor home towing a large cargo trailer did not seem too sensible, so Paul asked, "Do you have a spot available for us to camp here?"

We stayed in Milton for the next several days. We couldn't get over the friendliness and warmth of the people. We began to drive around the area, and we liked it.

We stopped at a realtor's office, and asked to look at a house we had spotted in a magazine advertising houses. We found it near Cantonment, Florida, and we loved the large Spanish house in the country with the neighbor's horses just beyond our back yard.

We remembered God's verse to us: *"Whither it seemeth good and convenient for thee to go, thither go!"*

Well, this seemed more than good and convenient! We signed papers to buy it just a couple days before

Christmas. All our belongings were still stored in the Michigan campgrounds. We celebrated Christmas Eve in our new house, sitting on the floor around the fireplace. We loved God and each other, and we felt the peace that God's angels had announced to earth nearly 2,000 years before.

Kathy and her husband loaded up all our furniture with the help of his brother and our faithful usher, Ron. They packed our things in the midst of a raging blizzard with the temperature way below zero. Then they delivered it all to us. (Don't ever believe that having eight kids isn't a tremendous blessing! We thank God for all of our children!)

We enjoyed settling in our new house.

Then Sunday came, and something totally unexpected happened to me. "God!" I cried. "I can't go to church!"

Attending church was a pleasure while we were traveling. But now we had bought a home. We would be living among these people. There would be new relationships formed with both true Christians and with wolves who merely covered up their true natures with sheep's clothing. We found we weren't ready for these new relationships!

Then we remembered God's clear commandment to not forsake assembling together with believers, especially in these last days.

We went to church, strictly out of obedience to God's Word. I shook and wept the whole way there—and I'm not usually one to either shake or weep.

We attended a nearby church that first Sunday morning. We heard an emotion-filled message from a charged-up preacher whose main theme was *"Purple*

Velvet Britches." We think the point he was trying to make was that women shouldn't wear makeup, jewelry, curls in their hair, or especially purple velvet britches. We six females all had on dresses, but we were wearing some makeup, jewelry, and my hair was neither long nor straight. We felt most of his message was directed straight at us, along with quite a few stares and smirks from the congregation. Since none of us, including Paul, even owned or desired to own a pair of those dreaded purple velvet britches, we decided to try out a different church that evening.

The owners of a nearby gas station invited us to their church, so we drove to *Cottage Hill Assembly of God* church on Sunday evening. The preacher walked toward us before the service, shook our hands, and said to Paul, "You're a preacher, aren't you?" Paul was startled.

We were hoping to hide that fact for the next few months at least, and Paul at this time in his life wasn't even sure what he was. In order to be a preacher, one had to preach. In order to pastor, one had to have a congregation. In order to be an evangelist, one had to evangelize. We were now in limbo, not knowing for sure what we were!

Paul answered hurriedly, "I just moved from Michigan. I ran a couple nursing homes there."

Now that was true—but it wasn't the whole truth!

Pastor Heiden answered, "I was sure you were a preacher. Well, anyway, we're glad to have you here."

God was in that church. The choir did not just sing, it ministered to hearts, and we wept as we listened to the anointed music. Pastor Heiden preached the Word of God fearlessly and powerfully, unctionized by the Holy Ghost. We enjoyed it all until the end of the message.

Then he said, "We're going to have our preacher from Michigan come up and close our service with prayer." And he looked straight at Paul.

Paul just sat there, so I jabbed him with my elbow. (Didn't God make elbows pointed and sharp for wives to jab husbands with when necessary?)

"Honey, he's talking to you!"

"I know. What shall I do? I can't go up there. I just can't stand behind a pulpit yet!"

"Yes, you can! I'll pray for you. You're going to have to. They're all waiting and staring."

Paul began the long walk up to the pulpit. He stood there for a moment, then began to pray. He prayed a few sentences, and then just broke down and wept. The people began weeping and praying too. But they didn't see the anguish behind Paul's tears—tears caused by a church that God had raised up totally destroyed; by severed friendships of people whom we loved; by brand new blood-bought souls who were now floundering in the midst of confusion; and by a pastor and his family with broken and torn hearts in dire need of the Savior's healing touch. Finally, he began praying again. Both we and the congregation were touched by God's special and sweet Presence.

We got back in our car after the service and the first words that Paul said were, "We can't go back to that church. I'm not ready for this yet."

I agreed. I wasn't either.

But God drew us back to those special people and their anointed pastor and his wife.

Pastor Heiden asked Paul to teach the adult Sunday School class the next Sunday. He reluctantly consented, and then regretted his decision for a week.

"I can't do it. I'm not ready!"

He taught. I sat and listened to the first part of the class. It was good. Then he stopped.

He looked straight at the adults gathered there and said, "God has just shown me there are people in this class who have been sent here by Satan to destroy this church. You hate your pastor and his wife, and, have determined to drive them from this church. I could point you out. I know who you are. God has a message for you who are trying to tear this flock apart, and He has sent me to deliver it."

Paul quit teaching and began to preach. Everyone felt a hush, as he implored the people to stand together, to forgive, and to be forgiven. The pastor's wife began to weep and praise God.

We learned later that Pastor Heiden's life had been recently threatened and it was confirmed that right here in this beautiful church there were the wolves who were placed in position by the destroyer to wreck yet another work of God.

Paul left church that morning with the words, "That's it! We can't go back to that church! I can't teach or preach yet. I'm simply not ready."

I agreed. We loved the church and we loved the people. But I still cried all the way to church. We needed healing and we needed more time before becoming involved in the ministry.

The final papers on our house were to be signed. The owner asked us to let the lawyer draw up the papers in a way that would not alert his bank of the sale. He didn't want his interest rate to be raised, and he was selling the house to us with owner financing. We would not consent, as it was dishonest, and would surely bring trouble in time. He refused to do it any other way, so we had to find another house.

Paul noticed an ad in the paper for a large house back in Milton. We looked at it one day, signed the papers to purchase it the next day, and moved in the following week. It was a beautiful, huge house, with access to two large catfish ponds. The girls all dove in the pool—in February! (Florida's February was hot to these Michiganders!)

Our move was a great relief to us. We were away from the church, and now could go hide among people who didn't know we had been in the ministry.

Our first Sunday in Milton, we attended another Assembly of God church.

The song service was lively, and we were thoroughly enjoying it, when right in the middle of the service, the song leader came back and stopped by our pew. "Do you folks sing?" he asked Paul.

We hadn't been singing loud! What made him ask that?

"Sometimes," Paul answered before he could think clearly.

The song leader returned to the front and announced we were going to sing! Now it was Paul's turn to jab me with his elbow. "Come on!" he said. "They're not taking no for an answer."

"I can't!"

I did.

We sang *He Touched Me.*

"Sing another one!" the preacher shouted when we finished.

We sang again.

And again.

"Now we're going to have our pastor friend preach for us! Come on, Brother!" were the next words we heard from Pastor Givens.

No one had told him Paul was a preacher. He had never seen us before!

Paul preached, and we gathered our family in the car following the service.

"That's it! Let's find another church."

We attended a small Assembly of God church in the country.

The pastor stood, looked at us for a moment, then asked us to sing.

This was getting ridiculous. We sang, and then the Lord anointed Paul and he just went ahead and preached. He figured he would be asked to anyway.

"I know what's wrong," he said as we got into our car. "I just figured it out this morning. We're going to the wrong churches. Assembly of God preachers hear from God. Now next Sunday, we are going to that Baptist church up the street from us. Baptist preachers go strictly by the Word, and there's no Bible verse that says, *"Attention! Paul Wilde is a preacher!"*

"Great idea!" I agreed.

The following Sunday found us in a Baptist church with about six-hundred people—a perfect place to hide.

Dr. Black was a great preacher. He had been a member of the *Hell's Angels* before finding Christ and he loved the Lord. He greeted us after the service with, "Aren't you the people who bought Geneva's house?"

"Yes," we replied warily.

"She told me all about you folks! She came to this church. She told me you sing and play the saxophone and preach! She read your book! Will you come and put on a concert in our church next Sunday evening? Take the whole service!"

We had given Geneva our book. She was moving to Kentucky, and we thought she'd be no threat to us in our new area! We were wrong.

Paul just gulped, and we looked at each other. It was finally beginning to dawn on us that God was not going to let us hide—even in a large Baptist church full of strangers.

We did the concert.

Our telephone rang the next week.

"This is Dr. Black. I heard it was a great service Sunday evening. I take revival meetings often. Could you fill in and preach for me next Sunday, both services, while I'm gone?"

Paul said yes, hung up the telephone, and breathed a prayer.

"Okay, God. We've received Your message. You still have a use for us. You obviously still want us in the ministry. Lead us, and we will follow, but You're going to have to give us strength."

211

Souls were saved at that Baptist church. Paul met them as they came forward to the altar. Many wept as they knelt and sought forgiveness from God through His Son and their new-found Savior, Jesus.

The deacons advised Paul after the service to let them handle those who responded to the call for salvation during the next service. They were not smiling.

Paul preached again and people came forward for salvation. They were immediately met by a deacon and handed a card and a pen and were told to fill in information on the card. Tears dried quickly as those who sought Christ filled in their cards. They talked to the deacons instead of to God. Then the deacons turned them toward the waiting congregation.

"This man (name) has come forward to join our church. All in favor of accepting him, say 'aye'." (Aye.)

"All not in favor, say 'nay'." (No nays.)

"Carried."

(Handshakes).

The man returned to his seat, not sure what had happened. He came seeking a Savior for salvation. He left, having become a member of a church.

Paul went home distraught. "What am I going to do? I'm not going to preach salvation just to have people fill out a card and get voted on by a bunch of people! If people could be saved by a vote, there would have been no reason for Jesus to shed His blood!"

We prayed and decided on what we considered to be a great plan. The next service, Paul preached about Jesus, and then asked all who wanted to be cleansed by His precious blood to stay right in their seats.

"Just bow your heads right where you are and pray this prayer:

Dear God, I come to You in the name of your only begotten Son, Jesus. I believe you sent Him to earth to save me from my sins. I ask for your forgiveness, and for the blood of Jesus to cleanse me from all my sins. Jesus, come and be my Savior, my Lord, and my King. I invite you into my heart, and into my life to live and reign. Amen."

Paul then asked those who had prayed that prayer to confess Jesus before men by coming forward. They came, weeping and praising God.

The deacons met them with a scowl, and we could feel the tension building. They went through their card ceremony, but this time, tears were not erased. These people had met Christ and were rejoicing!

Needless to say, we didn't get invited back to that church. In fact, Dr. Black has moved on too. But the greatest tragedy of all is that Jesus Christ is not really welcomed there either. How dare a church substitute itself for the living Christ and His salvation? The function of the church, the Bride of Christ, is to point people, not to herself, but to her Beloved.

We knew now with no doubts that we couldn't do anything but minister Christ and His salvation to people. God had left the fire of His gospel message still burning within us, and all the devil had done had not quenched it.

We mailed out letters with a copy of this book to two-hundred Assembly of God pastors, telling them we were available for evangelistic services. Our calendar began to fill with dates. We made arrangements to home school our girls and we began to travel. We held meetings in Pennsylvania, Texas, Alabama, and across Florida.

One day, we received a telephone call between meetings. It was from a pastor whose church we had been to. He told us that he, his wife, and a member of their church would be at our house for a visit at noon. We had food, but not enough to prepare a meal for company. So I sent the girls to the grocery store with a list. "Now don't spend too much," were my parting words to them. "Just get what is on the list."

They didn't spend too much, but it was enough to overdraw my checking account. On top of that, I couldn't believe the size of the ham Janet had bought. I didn't know they made them that small! First I prayed over it with the girls, and then I took practical steps. "This isn't going to feed more than four people, and there will be ten of us," I told the girls. "Well, here's what we'll do. Wait for our company to eat, before you take a piece of ham." I warned my husband, "One piece only.

They arrived, and we sat down to eat. (Now this doesn't make too much sense, even as I write it, but what miracle makes sense?)

We all ate ham until we were stuffed, and there was a plate full of ham that looked fuller than when I first served it. We ate ham again that evening, and I still had a container left over! The girls couldn't believe it. "Mom," they said, "this is impossible. This is a miracle just like the widow who fed Elijah, herself, and her son for many days with just enough food for one meal!"

There was still the problem of our checking account. After dinner, the preacher asked Paul to show him our place. They walked outside, around the property, and into the workshed. "Where did you get these things?" the preacher asked, pointing to old farm equipment and tools.

"They were here when I bought the place," Paul answered.

"Will you sell them to me?"

When he left, his car was packed full, leaving barely enough room for his wife and guest—and we had a check for over $300!

Our girls' faith was strengthened by that incident. They knew God took care of us. They had heard of the miracles that had happened when they were little, and now they were experiencing them first-hand. But they still weren't up to believing that God would take care of them and their own personal needs.

They got together one day, made themselves a list of what they felt were dire needs, and presented it to me. "We really need these things, Mom," they said.

"You're going to have to give this list to the Lord," I said, handing it back to them. "He will give you what you need."

"Nobody is going to give us girls money," they cried.

They complained and griped, but finally they grudgingly consented to pray for their needs. I figured it would be highly unlikely that God would honor their faith, because it was sadly lacking.

We went to Panama City, Florida for a revival the following week. During the final service there, Pastor Bay said, "I've been feeling led by God all day to do something special tonight. These five Wilde girls have been a tremendous blessing to our revival meeting. They have brought area teens that they met in the park in to the meetings. They have sung, befriended everyone, and prayed at the altar with our young people. And I want them to come forward and stand, and I want you to come give them a special appreciation offering."

Our girls looked at each other and then at me. They couldn't believe their ears. No one but God knew of their prayers. No church had ever taken an offering for them before or since. They learned that God hears and answers the prayers of all His people, and that lesson in faith was one they will never forget.

Needless to, say, the next day found us shopping!

Paul had made only one stipulation to God when we resumed His work, and I wholeheartedly agreed with it.

"Lord, we will go where you lead. However, don't ask me to pastor again. You surely realize I am not a pastor. I am an evangelist."

He then made this statement to me: I will *never* pastor again. And if I would, which I wouldn't, I would pastor in a huge city. I will *never* pastor a church in a small town."

I agreed with a hearty *Amen!*

God must have just chuckled and shook His head as He looked at our future.

3

Lovest thou me more than these? He saith unto him,
Yea, Lord; thou knowest that I love thee. He saith unto
him, Feed my lambs. (John 21:15)

We mailed out a letter to all our friends telling them
of our move from Michigan and giving them our
new address. One day, between revival meetings, our
doorbell rang and Del stood at our door. He was the
rodeo man we mentioned earlier whom we had won to
the Lord in Michigan.

"What are you doing here?" Paul asked.

" I live only an hour's drive from you, over in Alabama,
I got your letter this week, and drove over," Del
answered. "Come to our church and hold a revival
meeting! I attend *Bon Secour Assembly of God Church.*"

Paul told Del to see if his pastor wanted him to come.
A few days later, Del called back to tell us Pastor Wil-
hams wanted us to come.

We had a great meeting. Chuck, a member of *Calvary
Baptist Church* in Foley, attended the meetings.

"Come to our church," he said.

"I will if your pastor wants me to come."

"We don't have a pastor. We haven't had one for
quite awhile now. We do have an interim pastor."

"Have him call me if he wants me to come."

He did call, and dates were set for a revival in a
Southern Baptist church in Foley, Alabama.

There was very little response those first services. The people were warm and friendly, but we didn't see a move of God in response to Paul's messages.

Our second day in Foley, there was a loud banging on our trailer door. I hurriedly opened it to: "Get off this church parking lot with your trailer! We don't allow trailers here!" I quickly sent the city official into the church to Paul, where he said, "You've got just one hour to get this trailer moved!"

Paul called the interim pastor, who called the mayor, who called the inspector to tell him it was all right for evangelists to park their trailers at churches just for a few days of meetings. We weren't too sure we were welcome in this town.

The last day of the meetings, the organ player knocked on our trailer door. "I feel spiritually empty," he confessed. "Preacher, what is it that I need?"

Paul answered, "If you are truly born again and still feel empty, you need to be refilled with the Holy Ghost. All God's people need to be refilled from time to time —Methodists, Nazarenes, Pentecostals... and Baptists too." He showed him from the Scriptures that the disciples were filled with the Holy Ghost on the day of Pentecost. Then they went out doing the works of Christ, preaching, witnessing, and working miracles. They suffered persecution, were imprisoned, threatened, and warned to stop speaking the name of Jesus.

A short time later, in Acts, chapter 4, we find these same disciples praying for boldness to continue to work for the Lord. They prayed together, and again the place was shaken and again they were all filled with the Holy

Ghost, and they went out to preach God's Word and to do God's works with new power and boldness.

"Do you remember the story Jesus told us about the ten virgins?" Paul asked. "The reason five were wise is because they refilled their lamps when they ran out of oil. Just as a car needs to be filled and refilled with gas to keep traveling and a lamp needs to be filled and refilled with oil to keep giving light, we need to be filled and refilled with the Holy Ghost to continue to do the work of God."

"That's it! I can see it! This is what I've needed. Can we pray right now together?"

They prayed, he received a fresh touch and infilling simply by asking for it, and he left rejoicing. But just before he left, he turned to Paul and said, "We all need this. Our church needs this. Will you preach this to us tonight?"

Paul agreed, and God blessed. When he opened the altar call for those who were born again but needed to be refilled with the Holy Ghost, young and old, men and women literally poured from their seats and down the aisles. They knelt at the front of the church, filled the front few pews, knelt around the organ and piano benches, all asking God for a refilling, a fresh touch from His throne. And God answered their cries, and poured the oil of His Spirit upon them. It was beautiful.

We returned to Milton, and our telephone began to ring.

It was people calling from Foley.

"We don't have a pastor. We want you to come to our church and be our pastor."

"Pastor?!? Me pastor in Foley? I'm sorry, but no. You have a beautiful town, you're great people, but I am an evangelist, not a pastor."

We continued our travels. In between our meetings, our telephone kept ringing.

"We need you here in Foley!"

And finally...

"We're voting on you next week in our church!"

"What?!?"

"We're voting on you. Our congregation has this privilege, because the pulpit committee still hasn't called a pastor. We've been without one now for over a year."

Paul replied, "I guess I can't stop you from voting. But I want you to know that even if you vote for me to be your pastor, I can't come. I am an evangelist, not a pastor."

He repeated that last statement to me after hanging up the telephone. "I am an evangelist. It's great that they all want me to come, but I will never pastor again. Never!"

Just before the vote, our telephone rang again.

A dignified voice Paul had not heard before said, "The congregation has put your name up as our possible pastor. The church board needs to talk to you."

"I do not plan to pastor a church, even if voted on."

"We need to talk to you. We would like to come to your house."

"When?"

"This evening."

Their verdict following their talk with Paul was, "He is not a Southern Baptist."

They were right.

The weather was terrible the night of the vote, but a crowd gathered in spite of the weather. Some members who had faithfully attended the church for over sixteen years met other members for the first time that night. They had been contacted and asked to come and vote against Paul. The board was just as insistent as Paul that he was not going to pastor.

Just before the vote, a board member stood and said, "Whoever votes for Paul Wilde to pastor this church will be asked to leave the church."

Paul lost by two votes.

The same board member stood after the count was announced. "Those who voted for Paul Wilde as pastor and were previously asked to leave, we have decided to let you stay."

They left.

Our telephone rang.

"What are we going to do? They told us all to leave, then they told us we could stay after all, but we left."

"Go back," Paul said.

"No."

"Find another church."

"No. We will end up in all different churches if we do that."

"I don't know what you're going to do."

"We want you to come and be our pastor."

"No."

"Will you just come and meet with us and help us decide what to do?"

"Yes."

Over thirty of us gathered in a home that evening. We prayed and talked. They were all determined there was going to be a church with Paul as their pastor.

Paul was just as determined there wasn't going to be a church with him as their pastor.

It was finally agreed that they would rent a small day care center for the next couple Sundays before we left for Texas for revival meetings in Waco and Thornton. And Paul would preach for those two Sundays.

Our first Sunday in *Loving Care Day Care Center*, women and children sat in tiny chairs, most of the men and boys stood against the wall in back, and I was handed an organ with a few keys and fewer chord buttons. And... the Lord came. Souls were saved, backsliders restored, the music was true praise and worship. This was revival, and people crowded in to experience it—and we left for Texas.

Paul didn't tell me the prayer he prayed on our way to Waco. The church we were going to was a large one, and our meetings would begin on Easter Sunday morning. Posters had been hung all over the city, over fifteen-hundred invitations had been mailed, and Paul prayed, "Lord, if you are asking me to pastor a church in Foley, Alabama, I want you to show me. If this is your will, let this meeting in Waco be a disaster."

He knew he was safe. We already knew this would be a tremendous meeting. He had talked to the pastor by telephone, and the pastor was expecting a great move of God. The meetings were better advertised than most, and the church would be packed with the Easter-Christmas crowd who needed salvation. Paul knew when he prayed that token prayer that going to Foley would be settled once and for all. This meeting was destined to be one of our greatest!

We arrived in Waco on Saturday, and called the parsonage. No one was home. We parked at a gas station and Paul repeatedly called, but still no answer. Paul was getting restless, as it was getting later, and he likes to get his equipment set up in a church, check for sound, and get the trailer parked. Finally, the pastor's wife answered the telephone and told us how to get to the church.

A choir was there, taking a break during a practice session. None of them paid any attention to us, but finally Paul stopped one long enough to say, "I'm Paul Wilde, the evangelist."

Silence.

"Is your pastor here?"

"He's over there," nodding to a man with a tape measure in his hands.

Paul walked over to him.

He just kept measuring.

"Hello! I'm Paul Wilde. Are you Pastor _____?"

"Yes. But as you can see, I am busy measuring right now."

"Yes. I see that."

"Just go sit down and I'll talk to you when I finish measuring."

Paul sat down and watched him measure the precise distance between each row of folding chairs. It was a big church, and it took quite awhile. Finally, he came over to Paul. "I'm finished."

"If you don't mind," Paul said, "I'll just go ahead and set up my sound equipment."

"Wait! Don't be setting it up at all until after tomorrow morning's service. We are expecting a crowd, and our choir has decided to do a cantata tomorrow morning. You can preach when we're done. Don't be singing or playing. And have everything wrapped up in thirty minutes, from start to finish."

"Okay."

Paul came back to the trailer.

"Did you meet the pastor, Honey?"

"Yes. After he finished measuring."

"Measuring. Okay. Well, are you going to set up your equipment?"

"I was asked not to."

Paul preached the Word of God to a packed church that Easter Sunday morning. He gave the altar call. No one moved. No one even looked like they wanted to move.

That afternoon, the church telephone rang. It was the Foley bunch. "We had a great service this morning! Over sixty people crowded in! The singing evangelist you sent us did great. God really moved! Hurry back to Foley! We need you to be our pastor!"

Well, at least God was moving in Foley.

Sunday evening we sang, Paul played the saxophone, and he preached. He may as well have preached to stones.

After church, a group of young people and adults asked our girls to go to a restaurant with them. They were always eager to meet new friends, so they readily consented. We wondered if we were supposed to go along, when one man looked our way as he was getting into his car and yelled, "You can come too if you want to!"

We went.

The pastor and his wife were sitting in a booth. I hadn't yet met her, so we went to slide in and join them.

"Our friends usually sit here, and we were waiting for them," she said coldly. "However, you may sit here."

We quickly apologized and went to another table. Oh, well. At least our girls were meeting some people.

The following afternoon, we went to the church to practice. I played the organ, being careful to leave the settings just as I found them.

Just before the service, the pastor's wife (who I still hadn't met) went to the organ. She turned, facing the people, took her makeup from her purse, and made up her face. The girls and I stared, fascinated. We'd never seen an organist begin her prelude with a make-over. During the service, I accompanied one of Paul's saxophone numbers on the organ instead of the piano. The next day the organ was shut and locked!

Paul continued to preach to stones.

This was a disaster of a meeting, to say the least. Wednesday's service was a repeat of the others. We loaded our equipment, preparing to leave. (I did meet the pastor's wife just a few minutes before we left. She hadn't said hello during the past five days, but she did tell me good-bye with considerable relief.) The pastor came to Paul just before we pulled out and said, "I just don't know what's wrong with me. I don't normally act like I have this week. I'm sorry, but I can't explain what's happened, because I don't know myself."

Paul could have told him, but he was careful not to.

We went on to Thornton and had revival in a humble little church with wooden floors and wooden benches. The pastor received a salary of fifty dollars a week, and he gave fifteen of that to his adult Sunday School teacher for gasoline expenses. The most surprising thing about the Thornton meeting was that some of the stones from Waco drove over an hour's drive to attend the services and were both revived and saved! We reached more people from Waco in Thornton than we did in Waco!

It wasn't until our drive back east, that Paul told me about his prayer. I was horrified.

"Please don't ever pray that way again! That Waco meeting was awful! You could have asked God to show you some other way whether you are supposed to go pastor at Foley!"

Then it hit me.

"You mean we're going to Foley?"

We stopped at Foley on our way to Milton. We were greeted enthusiastically.

"How were your meetings in Texas?"

We changed the subject.

"Are you coming to pastor now?"

Paul answered, "Look. We can't keep meeting in a day care center with the men standing during services. If you can find a building we can use, maybe we will come.

A few weeks later, *New Life In Christ Church* of Foley, Alabama, owned a nice brick church and a small house on a beautiful piece of land visible from the main highway that runs through Foley. So much for making stipulations to God and informing Him what we would never do. God had provided as only He can. We knew now Foley was exactly where we were supposed to be and pastoring was exactly what we were supposed to do.

The church had been an Apostolic church. Its attendance was down to less than ten people. The elderly pastor desperately wanted to move. The women who went there just as desperately wanted him to move. They all wanted the church to remain a church. They told Paul, "If you will pastor here, you can have the church. Just take over the payments of $185 a month on the mortgage, $26 a month on the vacuum cleaner and pay the payments on the balance of $1,600 on our new air conditioning system. And here's the utility bill for this month of $135. And here's the deed to the church."

We registered the deed in the name of the new church, and could scarcely believe what God had done. The hymnals were in the pews, the dishes were in the kitchen, the piano was in place—everything was waiting for us to move in. We went to the bank to see how much remained to be paid on the mortgage. The balance due was $5,500. The total cost of our new church, the three bedroom house, the vacuum cleaner and the new air conditioning unit came to $7,400. It was appraised at $184,200.

We named our church *New Life In Christ Church* because we had heard repeated time and time again since coming to Foley, "I feel as if I have new life!"

Paul told them, "And you do. That new life is in Christ. Let's call our new church *New Life In Christ*.

Paul again cancelled all his revival meetings he had booked and the traveling evangelist again became a pastor.

But were we ready to pastor again?

We weren't quite sure, but if God led us here, surely He would give us the strength and grace to endure the pressures involved in pastoring.

He had been slowly but surely restoring both of us. One day as Paul listened to a message by James Robinson, God revealed bitterness in his heart against those who had driven us from our ministry in Muskegon. As Paul wept, our Great Physician performed surgery. It was painful, but he emerged with new spiritual health, love, and forgiveness. When Paul shared his experience with me, I too searched my heart, and found many things I needed Christ to remove. We had both discovered that God surely does *"heal the broken in heart, and bind up their wounds"* (Psalm 147:3).

We moved to Foley, a small town, but one surrounded by over 35,000 people, located just ten miles from the snow-white beaches of the Gulf of Mexico and situated between Pensacola, Florida and Mobile, Alabama.

God had replaced the dread of pastoring again with an excitement to begin our new work. We knew He was leading, we were following, and there is nothing that gives as much peace and joy to a minister than knowing that he is right in the center of God's will.

4

God forbid that I should glory, save in the cross of our Lord Jesus Christ, by whom the world is crucified unto me, and I unto the world. (Galatians 5:14)

We have been in Foley nearly six years now. God has been here with us. A few weeks ago, Malcom, one of our guitar players, said, "We're spoiled here. Souls are saved continually. I couldn't stand to go to a church where nothing is happening after being here."

And there has been a continual revival. Our people have learned that Christianity is not dull and that God is still a miracle-working God.

Several of us gathered together one Saturday to put a new roof on the church. It was partially done, when it started to rain. Marilyn, our church treasurer, was on the roof. (She couldn't stand not to be in the middle of everything, she was so excited about the church.) She got on the top rung of the ladder to climb down, and she fell to the blacktop beneath her. She lay on her back moaning, blood seeping from her mouth and her ears. She could not move and was in excruciating pain. We called an ambulance, stood over her with umbrellas, and Paul laid hands on her and asked God for a miracle. Marilyn immediately felt the healing touch of God as warmth enveloped her body and her pain instantly left. She was taken by ambulance to the hospital, but was released with no injuries.

One of the greatest healings took place in the hearts

of Paul, myself, and our five girls. God used the love of these special people in Foley to heal our internal wounds. We learned anew that *"The Lord is good to all: and his tender mercies are over all his works"* (Psalm 145:9).

We learned that if the pastor loves his people, the people love their pastor and his wife, love one another, and they all love the Lord, it is nearly impossible for the devil to destroy the church.

We were warned repeatedly by other pastors, "Enjoy yourself while the honeymoon lasts! It will soon be over!"

Now Paul and I have been married for nearly thirty years, and our honeymoon is not over yet! Our love for one another grows with the years. So we simply haven't accepted the fact that the love in our church cannot continue too!

Yes, there have been problems. When the devil tried to destroy through his age-old device of discord, Paul at first didn't want to face it head-on.

Then I, who seldom dream, dreamed. I saw a crew of workers building a large building. They hammered, nailed, and sawed vigorously all day long. Then they went home. Night came, and a second crew arrived. They wrecked everything that had been built during the day. And God spoke, *You cannot have a building crew and a wrecking crew on the same site. Nothing will ever be accomplished.*

As Paul and I discussed the dream, I remembered a poem I had read years before.

MY ROLE

I saw them tearing a building down,
A gang of men in a busy town;
With a ho-heave-ho and a lusty yell,
They swung a beam and a sidewall fell.

I asked the foreman, "Are these men skilled
As the men you would hire If you had to build?"
He laughed and said, "No, indeed!
Just common labor is all I need.
I can easily wreck in a day or two
What builders have taken a year to do."

I asked myself as I went my way,
Which of these roles have I tried to play?
Am I a builder who works with care
Measuring life with the rule and square?
Or am I a wrecker who walks the town,
Content with the labor of tearing down?

We confronted the wrecking crew. They did not repent, but they did leave the site, and work went on undisturbed.

We went to the Christmas parade, our first Christmas spent in Foley. We'd never attended one in Michigan! Nobody marches in six foot snowdrifts!

At the end of the parade, Roy Amos ran to Paul. "Pastor, they're going to burn crosses!"

"What? Why?"

Paul and Roy hurried to the city park, and Paul noticed four crosses and in front of them a circle. A man in a white robe and women in black robes with black eye masks and hoods stood in front of them. Then the circle and the crosses were set aflame. Foley's high school band was there playing, but as the crosses burned, a few of the Christian members put their instruments down as the rest of the band played.

Paul asked the man in the white robe, "Why are you burning crosses?"

The man looked directly at Paul. "You're not from here, are you?"

"No. What difference does that make? Why are you burning crosses in front of all these people?"

"You don't understand. You're not a Southerner. I'll talk to you later."

"Yes. We will talk later," Paul replied.

We checked the local newspaper with the schedule of Christmas festivities. It announced the lighting of the Christmas tree and the lighting of the crosses. We thought that was rather misleading as the Christmas tree wasn't burned up, but the crosses were!

Paul was really upset. "The children of Foley should not be watching crosses burned during the Christmas celebration."

We wrote a letter that was printed in the *Onlooker*, our Foley newspaper, as follows:

Dear Editor.

I was shocked and horrified as I stood in the park following the Christmas parade in Foley, and witnessed the burning of the crosses. I believed that Christmas, as celebrated by the res idents of Foley, was to commemorate the birth of our Lord and Savior, Jesus Christ. This same Jesus gave His life on a cross that men might be saved. The Word of God says, "For the preaching of the cross is to them that perish foolishness; but unto us which are saved it is the power of God." It is this same Jesus whose birth among men is being honored during this Christmas season. Why then the burning of the crosses?

I received varied explanations in answer to my question.

"It is an old Scottish custom. It has nothing to do with Christ, but originated before his birth."

As to its being an old custom, God's Word says, "Walk ye not in the statutes of your fathers, neither observe their judgments, nor defile yourselves with their idols: I am the Lord your God; walk in my statutes, and keep my judgments, and do them" (Ezekiel 20:1819).

Then we heard, "It is a ceremony to bring in the New Year."

Why should the burning of crosses be symbolic of the new year? Do we really want Foley to welcome the new year by destroying crosses?

God's Word declares unto us the gospel, which is, "Christ died for our sins according to the scriptures; and that he was buried and that he rose again the third day." The Apostle Paul boldly stated, "Though we, or an angel from heaven, preach any other gospel unto you than that which we have preached unto you, let him be accursed... for I neither received it of man, neither was I taught it, but by the revelation of Jesus Christ" (Galatians 1:8, 12).

Do we in Foley want to be accursed by God for mocking His death by destroying crosses, while professing to honor His birth?

234

Then we heard, "It is a Southern custom."

It seems strange that every native Southerner I talked to denied this vehemently and was appalled at such a charge.

We were told that this custom was around before Jesus was.

God's Word proclaims that Jesus Christ is the Lamb slain from the foundation of the world! Ephesians 3:9 says that "God created all things by Jesus Christ!" Jesus Himself claimed, "I am Alpha and Omega, the beginning and the end ing, saith the Lord, which is, and which was, and which Is to come, the Almighty."

Jesus Christ is the Beginning! His life did not begin when the Virgin Mary conceived of the Holy Ghost! That was only the beginning of His life on this earth! This custom could not have originated before Christ! He is the Beginning!

In Bible times, there were "enemies of the cross of Christ whose end is destruction." Paul both warned and wept because of them!

Perhaps many who were responsible for the Christmas festivities were unaware that crosses would be burned. Perhaps our local newspaper innocently misled the public as it described the events. It stated, "Three giant crosses will be lighted as a symbol of the starting of a new year." The same article referred to the "lighting of the big Christmas tree." The crosses were burned. The lights on the tree were plugged in.

It has been and always will be Satan who despises the cross that marked the beginning of his destruction. The cross Is hated and despised by some, ignored and considered foolish to others, but "unto us which are saved it is the power of God."

Crosses are erected in cemeteries over the gravesites of soldiers who have died a sacrificial death for their countries. There is no city in America that would allow men to burn these crosses, because we honor the men whom the crosses represent.

235

Christians honor the Lord Jesus Christ, and the cross represents His sacrificial death for us.

It is a precious symbol to us of our Savior's death. It sickens us to watch it burn. We commend each member of the Foley High School band who put down their instruments during the cross burning ceremony, and refused to participate in such paganistic blasphemy.

We hope and fervently pray that our city officials will follow the example set by these fine young people and refuse to allow this devil honoring, Christ-defying ceremony to take place In Foley again.

Sincerely,

Paul Wilde

Pastor, New Life In Christ Church

Roy also wrote this letter that was printed in the *Onlooker.*

Dear Editor:

The traditional Christmas parade was a beautiful and colorful parade with its bands, scout troops, shriners, horses, and floats. Our church, the New Life In Christ Church, had a float in the parade. This is the first parade that I have witnessed in some years. Everything seemed to go very smoothly and the parade climaxed at the Foley Park directly across the street from the LePhone Shop and the recently restored Old Magnolia Hotel which are owned by John M. Snook of the Gulf Telephone Company.

The audio of the PA system was poor, but I heard something about burning. I wedged my way through the crowd and before my eyes was a circle about six feet in diameter with flares on it and directly behind it were four crosses constructed of steel pipe and wrapped and bound with burlap that was treated with something flammable.

According to the editor of the Onlooker, Mr. Snook was the organizer of this event. I became a born again Christian on August 7, 1985, and I could not just stand and watch the cross burning. I ran back up the street and told my pastor what was happening.

We hurried back to the park, just as the crosses were being set on fire. We questioned a police officer who was standing by, but did not get any answers from him.

I pointed out Mr. Snook to Pastor Wilde, and he walked over to him and attempted to question him about the activities. When asked why he was burning crosses, Mr. Snook replied that it was a southern tradition.

Well, I have lived in the south all my life and burning crosses is certainly not a southern tradition.

Pastor Wilde pointed out to Mr. Snook that burning crosses and the circle of fire was an act of witchcraft and a form of Satan worship. Mr. Snook said It was brought over to this world by our forefathers. I don't remember anything about the Pilgrims burning crosses! Then Mr. Snook just smiled, and said that Wilde had not been in the South long enough, and turned and walked away.

I recognized another police officer at the scene as one of my life-long friends. I asked him why crosses were being burned in the public park. He replied that there was nothing wrong with it. Pastor Wilde told him that it was an act of witchcraft and satan worship, and he told Pastor Wilde that he had better go study up on the history of Christianity and then advised us that if we did not like what we were seeing to leave.

Our problem was not that just we were seeing crosses burn, but that the crosses were set up about fifty feet south of the Santa Claus line where all the little children were lining up! If these children see crosses burned every Christmas, they will believe this is part of normal Christmas celebrations!

The cross is sacred to me. It is to be honored, because Jesus died so I could be saved and have eternal life. A copy of this letter will be sent to our city officials, requesting them not to allow this act on public property again.

If they don't prevent it, they'd better build a bigger jail, because if this act is repeated in our city park, I and many other Christians will be on hand to protest and prevent it from happening.

Very Sincerely,

Roy A. Amos

Mr. Snook was interviewed by the *Onlooker*, and the following article was printed as a result of that interview:

CROSS BURNING ANCIENT PAGAN RITUAL

The burning of the crosses in Foley Park following the Christmas Parade last Saturday may have offended some people, but according to John Snook, organizer of the event, it only offended them because they are unaware of ancient Scottish and southern traditions.

The burning of crosses was part of ancient pagan rituals celebrating winter solstice long before the birth of Christ, Snook said and the celebration of Christmas coincides with the ancient traditions of these rituals.

"It is a tradition brought from Scotland to the south and is similar to the burning of bonfires on the levy in New Orleans at Christmas," he said.

When asked if he knew that the burning of crosses and circle of fire might be construed as satanic or Ku Klux Klan inspired, he replied, "It is not meant to be satanic. It simply symbolizes the merger of light and life."

The *Onlooker* contacted the Mobile Public Library, and according to sources there, pagans celebrated the seasonal change around December 21 or the summer solstice. This celebration occurred before the birth of Jesus Christ and is now called a pagan ritual.

When Christians began to develop a celebration for the birth of Christ, they did not know the exact date of his birth, according to library sources. The library sources say early Christians then decided to have the celebration of the birth of Christ on the same date as the old custom of the celebration of winter solstice.

Snook says he was celebrating in a manner similar to the way those people celebrated before Christ's birth, and according to him, it is just a recognition of a part of history.

"We have been doing the some thing for 30 years now. I don't understand why everyone is so upset this year," Snook said.

City Magistrate, Joe Bischoff said that this year's parade was the biggest celebration in Foley's history and that it was probably the "newcomers" to the area that were unaware of this yearly ceremony and were upset by it. "We've had it every year since I came here in 1969," he said.

"Lighting of crosses and bonfires is an old custom that symbolizes the merger of light and life and is really a part of new year ceremonies," Snook said.

According to Bischoff, the ceremony in question was meant to be part of a festival, a celebration of the old customs of the area and in Europe.

Snook and Bischoff said that if the ceremony offends that many people that it will not be held on public property again, but will be held on Snook's private property.

Shortly after the letters were printed, Roy telephoned Paul. "The Kiwanis Club sponsors the Christmas activities each year, and they have invited me to come to their dinner meeting Tuesday to tell them why I object to burning crosses in our city park. They said I could bring along a guest. Would you come and pray for me?"

They attended the meeting, Roy to speak, and Paul to pray. Following dinner, Paul was shocked to hear: "We have Rev. Wilde with us today. He is going to tell us why he objects to burning crosses."

Paul turned to Roy, and whispered, "Roy, you said you were supposed to speak, not me!"

Roy whispered back, "I was! But go right ahead! And I will pray for you!"

"Paul," the speaker continued, glancing at his watch, "we will give you exactly three minutes to state your views."

"Roy had better be praying," Paul thought as he stood to speak. He had no idea what he was going to say. Then he glanced at the flag, and God gave him a thought.

"I was impressed as I watched you all stand before your meeting and pledge allegiance to the flag of the United States of America. Every one of you spoke those words with respect and honor, and I commend you for that. Our flag represents our freedom to us, and that freedom was bought with a tremendous price. Some of you, some of your fathers, your brothers, and your uncles paid for this freedom and liberty with their blood. Because of their sacrifice, the flag is precious to us."

Then Paul changed his tone. "How would you like it if I walked over to this flag, tore it from its stand, stomped on it, and set it a fire? Oh, you're looking angry at even such a suggestion. And rightly so. You don't want the flag desecrated, because it's a cherished symbol to you."

"Even so, the cross is a cherished symbol to every Christian. Jesus Christ gave His life and shed His blood on the cross to obtain freedom and liberty for me. Because of His sacrifice, the cross means something to me. I cannot stand by silently and watch it burned."

Paul sat down in less than three minutes.

The guest speaker for the day was forgotten, as the men discussed the issue.

"This is a custom brought over from Europe!"

Paul spoke up. "Many customs were brought over from Europe. This is one that should have stayed there."

Finally they voted, and the decision was made. Crosses would not again be burned on public property during events the Kiwanis Club was sponsoring.

It was a victory to put to an end a pagan custom that had gone on in Foley unchallenged for thirty years. But the real victory will be when the cross will become precious to those who desire to burn it, and they too will enjoy the freedom from sin that our Savior paid for on that old rugged cross.

H. L. and Mary helped us with the float we entered in the parade the second year. We built a stable, a manger, and made beautiful costumes. We had a flat bed with Joseph, Mary, a battery operated moving doll placed in the manger, a golden haired angel perched on top of the stable, wise men and shepherds placed off to the sides. We added two live sheep and a donkey, and painted "Wise Men Still Seek Him" across the sides. The crowds loved the float and the judges awarded it first prize. H.L. more than deserved the honor. Watching him chase the donkey and push, tug, and finally lift it onto the trailer was a whole lot of fun for everyone but H.L. The sheep were even worse than the donkey. He chased them all over our church parking lot, across the street, out of the ditch, and finally tackled them. We were all too busy laughing at him to help. The only one of us who wasn't laughing by the time the animals were tethered to the float was H.L. We still have all we need to enter that float again. But H.L. moved to northern Alabama, and we haven't been able to find anyone else who wants to go through all he did to let Foley know that Jesus truly is "the Reason for the Season."

Last Christmas we had a Christmas play. Our Elizabeth had the idea for the script. We portrayed a bag lady who arrived in a neighborhood and two families with two very different reactions to her during the Christmas season. Liz played the part of the bag lady, which came quite naturally to her. (We have always thought, when passing her bedroom, that being a bag lady has been her secret ambition.) She also got to burp in the play and to burp in public without being reprimanded was a real delight for our beautiful, fun-loving nineteen year old daughter. At the end of the play, Elizabeth was transformed into a radiant angel sent on a mission to earth to see how folks would treat her. The play was based on Hebrews 13:1-2: *"Let brotherly love continue. Be not forgetful to entertain strangers: for thereby some have entertained angels*

242

unawares." Our church was packed, and lives were challenged and changed. Many people told us that they saw their own self-centeredness in the play, and they went out to find a lonely or needy person to help, not by just handing him food or money, but by inviting him into their hearts, homes, and lives, and sharing with him their time and their love.

Our church filled with people of all backgrounds: Catholics, Episcopalians, Methodists, Baptists, Pentecostals, even some Mormons and Jehovah's Witnesses. And then there were many with no church background at all. We all met at the foot of the cross, and the bond that held us all together was Jesus and His love.

Paul taught foundation classes consistently to found people in the Word of God, and the church grew both numerically and spiritually.

We gave a lot of our time and efforts to teenagers. Our youth choir has sung in prisons, hospitals, streets, children and nursing homes, on television, city festivals, state parks, and in our studio—recording a tape. Each Saturday evening from six to nine, our teens get together for ministry, fun, and fellowship.

One man complained, "You're spending too much time with the youth!" How can a church give too much time to its young people? Our teens are not only our future pastors, song leaders, evangelists and Sunday School teachers, but we discovered that they are also a big part of our present church. They have a lot to offer and are a real blessing in our services. We have turned over some of our services to them, and they have preached the Word of God, testified, sung specials, prayed for our needs, and been a tremendous blessing. Most of life's major decisions are made during the teen years—education, career, marriage partner, taking the drink or the drug that leads to alcoholism or addiction, friendships—and our teens desperately need spiritual help and guidance during these crucial years.

A Baptist preacher called and invited us to his home for dinner. After grilling us steaks, he said, "I'd like to ask you just one question. How has your church grown so fast? What are you doing?"

Paul answered without hesitation, "We simply meet the needs of the people, and God blesses our labors. Sunday morning begins with our radio program, then continues with Sunday School and morning worship. Each Sunday afternoon we have three choirs practicing. On the second Sunday of the month we hold a 2:00 p.m. service at the nursing home. On Monday evenings about seventy children gather for Pioneers' Club. Others meet on Mondays for home Bible studies. Every Wednesday evening we have an on-fire service, with lively music, special numbers, testimonies and sermon. We have seen many people come to Christ during our Wednesday services. On Thursday evenings I teach the Bible Foundation Class to found new converts in the Word. On Friday evenings our Fellowship Hall is open for adults who desire Christian Fellowship. New converts who have spent their weekends in bars before they met Christ need to have a place to go to receive the strength that comes from being with other Christians. Saturday evenings are dedicated to our teenagers. We have a wonderful couple who spend their retirement years ministering to the needs of the elderly in our church and community. We hold church get-acquainted picnics and banquets for our Senior Saints. We pray for the sick and for special needs after each service. Our church pays tithes to a *Love Fund* and the money is distributed to people in the community with financial needs and to other ministries."

Paul continued, "When someone comes into church who is bound by alcohol, addictions, or is devil-possessed, we pray for their deliverance in the name of Jesus."

"We have Thanksgiving and Christmas dinners for people who do not have families to celebrate their holidays with. We have a party for children and teens on Halloween to keep them from getting involved in satanic practices. During spring break, when so many teens go to Gulf Shores to drink and party, we provide a camping trip for fun, fellowship, singing around bonfires, and Christian movies."

"I realize I alone cannot bring the people to perfection. According to Ephesians 4:11-12, *'Jesus gave apostles, prophets, evangelists, pastors and teachers for the perfecting of the saints, the work of the ministry, and for the edifying of the body of Christ.'* So we bring in many other ministers, and the people receive help from them."

"We work together as a body of Christ. The people do not expect Carolyn and I to do all the work. They go out and win souls, they pray for peoples' needs, they repair widows' houses, and they, uncomplaining, just do the work of God, whenever and wherever it needs doing."

Paul concluded, "We've been called to Foley to minister. A minister serves people. We simply try to meet the needs of people, and God blesses our efforts."

God does bless. Our church grows. We had removed the back walls to expand our seating capacity. We turned the house into Sunday School rooms. We built a pavilion for fellowship, and then enclosed it so we could use it year around.

We decided to build a new church right next to our old one. We met with a contractor and drew up plans for a building that would seat over five-hundred people on pews, and over eight-hundred people by setting up extra folding chairs.

Our bank turned down our application for our loan. We were wondering what to do, when a Vice President of an old and established Pensacola bank called us. We had never done business in Pensacola, and had not heard of the bank or the Vice President.

"The contractor you asked to build your church mentioned to the President of our bank that your church needs a loan. Please come over. We will give you the money you need."

Who but God would arrange to have a bank call us and ask to lend us money? We have been banking for thirty years, and have never heard of such a thing! With our God, nothing is impossible!

We opened August 5, 1990, and we have had beautiful services in it. Walt Mills came to preach and sing; the Dixie Echoes blessed us with their vibrant music. John Starnes ministered in song and word. Andy Bryan, an on-fire Baptist evangelist, inspired everyone and Billy Walker has both preached the Word and prophesied. In between all the special meetings have also been special meetings. Whenever God is present, the meeting is special. Souls have continually been saved, and we have been blessed with an ongoing revival.

Yes, we tire. The harvest is endless. As far as the eye can see in any direction, there is work to be done. There are no shortages of sinners to be saved, sick to be healed, captives to be set free, lonely to be befriended, or grieving to be comforted.

Someone said to us after reading our book, "You don't have to live by faith anymore."

We are still living by faith, and we praise our God for the way He cares for His people. We not only trust Him for our daily needs, but also for the needs of the church! We have carried the same principles we have learned to live by into our church—and they work!

A couple came to our church for several Sundays, and finally asked, "How are we supposed to give offerings in this church? You don't pass offering plates!"

Paul has replaced the custom of passing offering plates with putting two boxes at the back of the church. He, along with many Christians today, is tired of the emphasis put on money. We were in the hospital emergency room one night when a rowdy group of young men came in carrying one of their wounded who had overdosed on a combination of drugs and alcohol. The doctor jokingly said to us, "You don't want to take some of these home with you, do you?"

Paul answered, "I'll take them to church. I think they need help."

The doctor's face immediately sobered, and he said stiffly, "You don't want them in church. They don't have any money."

What a picture the world has of Christ's church!

The church should be in existence to minister to the poor and the needy. At least, that's how it all started two-thousand years ago, according to the Founder of the church, Jesus Christ!

Paul told our church board that he would like to omit passing offerings plates except for special singers and evangelists, a special offering for someone in the church or community who has a desperate financial need and once a month for our new church.

One board member objected, "Our offerings will fall to nothing!"

They didn't. They nearly doubled.

We not only are able to have a church that does not beg for money, but we no longer have to interrupt our services to receive an offering when the Holy Spirit is moving on hearts. Also, Paul often had forgotten all about the offering when the Lord was moving in our services, and our Treasurer would remind him after the service that we did have bills to pay! So the boxes at the back are working fine!

Yes, we're still living by faith. It was a big step of faith to build a new church. We do not have a church full of wealthy people. In fact, many are just barely keeping up with their bills. We have a church where anyone seeking a Savior and Christian fellowship can come in and not feel intimidated by others. The poor who cannot dress in the latest styles can come in and feel a warm and genuine welcome and acceptance. That's the beautiful thing about our Savior—He loves and accepts each one of us just as we are.

He demonstrated this recently to Marilyn, our church treasurer, in a very special way. Her brother lay dying of AIDS.

She visited him in Chicago. "Are you ready to die? Have you received Jesus Christ as your personal Savior?" she asked him.

He didn't respond,

She tried again later.

"Jesus loves you so much that He died for you. He loves you right now, just as you are. He is willing and waiting to forgive you for every one of your sins. He will cleanse you with His blood, make you His child, and welcome you into heaven at your death."

This time Michael prayed and found the joy and peace of heart that only receiving Jesus can bring.

Later he was moved to Wisconsin, where his assigned "Special Buddy" Theresa, said to him, "Are you sure you are ready to die?"

"I'm trusting my Savior, Jesus Christ," he replied.

She questioned him again, and he finally said, "Look! I'll send you a rainbow when I get to heaven!"

They laughed together. He died a short time later, and as the hearse was leaving the hospital carrying his ravaged body, a beautiful, brilliant rainbow in a nearly cloudless sky arched above the city. His family was called to come to the hospital. Marilyn was among them, as they stood with tear-filled eyes, viewing the end of the rainbow stopping right at Michael's hospital room. Pictures were taken of the rainbow. What a testimony of our Lord's saving grace!

The rainbow began with a promise and in Wisconsin another promise was given as a mute but powerful witness that **JESUS SAVES!**

Jesus said, *"All that come to me, I will in no wise cast out."*

We, as His people, want to be an extension of that promise. We welcome each one who truly wants to have God's touch on their lives. Jesus came to minister, not to the well, but to the sick; not to the righteous, but to the sinners.

Until our blessed Savior returns for His people, we will continue by His strength and grace to plant and sow His Word.

Our children are grown now. Suzy, our youngest is seventeen and the only one still home. She is a blessing, waking us up in the morning with her singing, and still singing praises to God when we go to bed. Our other seven are married, with families of their own, learning their personal lessons of living by faith.

The other day I answered my telephone to hysterical crying. One of our daughters cried, "Mom, I've made a mistake in my checkbook and I'm $4.00 overdrawn. I lost my job. My car is out of gas! My husband's paycheck is late, and we're out of food! We've been faithful giving to God and working for God. Living by faith doesn't work!"

I tried to settle her down. "Tell me exactly what you have left for food."

"Two boxes of augratin potatoes, a jar half-full of peanut butter, and a box half-full of grits. We're out of milk and bread."

I laughed. "God is not going to give you food until you eat your grits!"

Then she really howled! "Then I'm going outside to dump them right now! I hate grits! And this isn't funny! Living by faith like you wrote about just doesn't work!"

She paused a minute to sniffle. Then, "Oh, great! Now I've got company coming, and I'm crying!"

I heard her call out in a perfectly normal and dramatically changed voice, "Come in!"

Then I heard, "It's my friend... with bread, chicken, jam, hamburg.... Mom, she's brought a whole bunch of food!"

"Living by faith does work! It works!"

"Bye, Mom."

She also received a twenty dollar check in the mail that day to deposit in her checking account—and within a couple days had a new job!

What a blessing it is to see others begin to trust God!

After all God has done for us, we cannot help but tell others about His goodness. This book was written so that we can say with David, *"I have not hid thy righteousness within my heart; I have declared thy faithfulness and thy salvation: I have not concealed thy lovingkindness and thy truth from the great congregation"* (Psalm 40:10).

Perhaps the Lord blessed us with eight children so we could testify that God has more than abundantly provided for our family of ten when we put Him first in our lives. And if He can care for our family, He can surely care for yours! Few families are as large as ours today!

We can say with the Apostle Paul that through these years of serving God we have been *"troubled on every side, yet not distressed; perplexed, but not in despair; persecuted, but not forsaken; cast down, but not destroyed"* (II Corinthians 4:8-9).

We invite you to come to Foley, Alabama and visit us at New Life In Christ Church. You will find a church full of friendly people who love God and who are learning to live by faith so they can join us in telling you:

"Happy is he that hath the God of Jacob for his help, whose hope is in the Lord his God:

Which made heaven, and earth, the sea, and all that therein is: which keepeth truth for ever:

Which executeth judgment for the oppressed: which giveth food to the hungry. The Lord looseth the prisoners:

The Lord openeth the eyes of the blind: the Lord raiseth them that are bowed down: the Lord loveth the righteous:

The Lord preserveth the strangers; he relieveth the fatherless and widow: but the way of the wicked he turneth upside down.

The Lord shall reign for ever, even thy God O Zion, unto all generations. Praise ye the Lord." (Psalm 146:5-10)

Addendum II

*Y*ou are probably wishing this book would end, so you could get some sleep.

I have brought it to a close twice now. Then when another printing is needed, Paul and I say, "Wait! Before we print more books, we have to tell the people about some of the great things that have happened since the last printing!"

So many answers to prayers....

Our wonderful Father in heaven is so very, very good to us...

So, please settle back for just a few more minutes, and let me tell you in this second expansion how the Lord has continued to lead us on the road of faith.

The telephone rang.

"Are you Paul Wilde?"

"Yes."

"Did your wife write the book, *We've Come This Far by Faith?*"

"Yes, she did."

"I am calling from a bank in Virginia to inform you that someone wants to anonymously make a sizable donation to your ministry. If you do not have a stock broker, please open an account, and call me back so we can transfer stocks for you to sell."

We found a stock broker and opened an account, all the time wondering, "What is *sizeable*? Could this donation be as much as $10,000?"

I need to interrupt this story to tell you about our prayer warriors. When I wrote a new book, *Torchbearers*, I studied our tremendous Christian heritage of centuries past. I had never been much for studying history, so I approached the task of writing *Torchbearers* with dread. The work quickly turned into enjoyment! I found a spiritual feast was in store for me! Men, women, teenagers and children have faithfully carried the torch for Christ down through each century. While digging through old journals, letters, books and Bibles, I met desolate slaves, prosperous merchants, destitute failures, aged men, courageous women, fearless professors, helpless invalids, elderly women, sharp lawyers, drunken teenagers, mass murderers, hardworking housewives, dying men, respectable counts, sneering agnostics, vile blasphemers and despised priests. I found them in slave ships, hog pens, battlefields, prisons, Indian tepees, mansions, orphanages, forests and dungeons—all people that God turned into mighty torchbearers to carry His light to our sin-blackened world. What a heritage we Christians have!

I met Augustine, born back in 354 b.c. I was shocked to discover his generation was embroiled in a vicious debate about a practice taking place... *abortion*! As

Solomon said, there really isn't anything new under the sun!

I read with horror about the woman and six men who were set aflame in a city square in England in the late 1400's. Their crime was teaching their children the Lords prayer, the ten commandments and the Apostles' Creed in the English language. It makes our definition of persecution today pale into petty insignificance.

I almost felt like I knew Katie, a feisty little lady who wore her red hair tied up in pig tails, and kept a lively home for her husband, Martin Luther, and their ten children. I laughed, thinking about our own noisy home, when I learned that Martin had retreated to his study for some peace and quiet. After three days, Katie got disgusted when her husband was still locked up in his study. She tried in vain to coax him out. Finally she simply removed the study door from its hinges, and their brood had access to their father once again!

I realized Martin must have felt like every pastor does at times, struggling with a congregation grown complacent. But I don't know a pastor who took the drastic measures he did to shake them back awake.

"I refuse to preach to you," he thundered. "You remain godless! It annoys me to keep preaching to you!"

So he went on strike and refused to preach to the lukewarm bunch again until his shocked parishioners mended their ways.

He also grew weary and deeply discouraged at times, just like many of us do. But Katie would not allow that for long. One day he came home to hear her wailing. He found her dressed in mourning, her expression as black as her clothing.

"Katie, who died?"

She continued to sob, and we can almost see him bending over and giving her a shake.

"Katie! Tell me, Kate, who died?"

She finally was able to answer him through her wrenching sobs.

"Oh, Martin, God is dead! It is God who died! I can't bear it, for all his work is overthrown!"

He surely must have straightened up in shock! Then he became enraged.

"Katherina, that is utter blasphemy! God is not dead."

Her crying ceased abruptly. She stood and looked him straight in the eye.

"Martin," she said sternly, "you have been going around acting as if God is dead; as if God is no longer here to keep us. So I thought I ought to put on mourning to keep you company in your great bereavement."

Martin straightened up, but he did later confide to his friend, "If I should ever marry again, I would hew me an obedient wife out of stone."

I read the journal of faithful David Brainerd, who was born in Connecticut in 1718. Though weak and dying of tuberculosis, David literally crawled through dense forests and swamps to find villages where he could tell Indians about Jesus Christ. He struggled to learn the different Indian languages, but finally found an interpreter. (David had trouble even remembering kremmogkodonaltootiteavreganumeouash, the thirty-six letter word for question!) His interpreter was usually drunk, and David had no idea whether his message was being interpreted correctly or not. Just when David was thinking about giving up his ministry, his interpreter was saved and began to interpret his messages with a powerful anointing. Entire Indian villages turned to Christ. I hadn't known about the crowds of three to four-thousand Indians gathered in the fields and on the rolling hillsides of Eastern America, responding to the gospel with tears. Entire villages were transformed by the power of Christ. David often heard them praying and singing all night long. Angels collected his spent body at the age of only twenty-nine.

John Wesley was a torchbearer who made me feel lazy! He was 5'3" and weighed in at 128 pounds. His church was the great outdoors, and crowds of over 20,000 people lined the English hillsides. He preached over 40,000 sermons, wrote more than two hundred books, edited a magazine, compiled dictionaries in four languages, and composed a home medical handbook... all in his own handwriting. He traveled over 250,000 miles on horseback to tell people about Jesus—the equivalent of riding ten times around the world along its equator! At eighty-three years of age, John Wesley was discouraged because of his failing energy. He complained in his journal that he was no longer able to read or write more than fifteen hours a day without his eyes hurting. He regretted that he had to limit himself to only two sermons a day. And he confessed with shame that he had an increasing tendency to lie in bed until 5:30 a.m.

God set Annie Taylor ablaze for Him. She was nearly an invalid, suffering with a weak heart from her birth. Instead of calling her to an easy task, God sent her to one of the wildest and most rugged places on earth... Tibet. *(Since 1950, visitors traveling to Tibet must first pass a heart and lung test in Beijing!)* Annie trudged in bitter gales and frigid winds through snowdrifts, eating meals of raw goat or sheep. She learned her guide was a treacherous murderer. She slept in caves, tents and snowdrifts. When she finally reached Tibet, her first stop was the Buddhist monastery to tell the powerful lamas and their followers about her Savior. Many turned to Him for salvation.

It was a torchbearer who lived in the 1700's whose life literally transformed our church. Wealthy Count Zinzendorf, of Southeastern Saxony, turned his estate into a refuge for Christians fleeing from fierce persecution. On August 27, 1727, Count Zinzendorf began an around-the-clock prayer meeting with twenty-four couples who each prayed in shifts for one hour a day. Word spread about their unceasing prayer, and many joined them. Prayers began to ascend to God's throne at all hours of the day and night... from ships, islands, caves, cities, countryside and forests. The prayer meeting continued nonstop... for one-hundred years! During this time, the *Great Awakening* swept through England and America. Hundreds of thousands of souls were birthed into the Kingdom of God... all as a result of prayer without ceasing.

I was sharing this story with my Sunday School class one Sunday morning, when an excited new convert said, "Why can't we do that?" *Well... why can't we?*

So we did. Over one-hundred prayer warriors began to pray in shifts—around the clock—for over five years. Some prayed for fifteen minutes and others for an hour. All of us working together kept our prayer requests before the throne of God twenty-four hours a day!

One of the requests we took to our Father was for the mortgage of our church to be paid in full. There are so many things happening today with the microchips and computers that are swiftly leading our world into a new monetary system. Ultimately the coming cashless society will lead us right into the mark of the beast. We realize as Christians that tremendous economic upheavals could be just ahead. By having a debt free church, could our church doors remain open longer than they could if we were laden with debts? Being debt free could possibly give us more years to preach, win souls, baptize new converts and strengthen fellow Christians. Being debt free would definitely enable us to give more to missions and outreach ministries. Much of our money was going to pay interest on our huge mortgage!

Just months from the day we submitted this request, we were anxiously waiting to hear what *"sizeable"* meant. What an awesome God we serve!

Jesus left this promise to anyone who would follow Him: *"There is no man that hath left house, or brethren, or sisters, or father, or mother, or wife, or children, or lands, for my sake, and the gospels, but he shall receive* *an hundredfold **now in this time**, houses, and brethren, and sisters, and mothers, and children, and lands, **with persecutions**; and in the world to come eternal life"* (Mark 10:29-30).

Blessings... with persecutions....

Yes, persecutions do come with every blessing.

Before I tell you about the persecutions, let me tell you about another blessing that took place deep in the rain forest of Hawaii.

2

For this purpose the Son of God was manifested, that he might destroy the works of the devil. *(I John 3:8)*

$\mathcal{I}$t was just another Wednesday evening service ...or so we thought.

Then why was one of our deacons wearing an Hawaiian shirt with a flower in his lapel?

Paul parked the car.

"Are you going to Hawaii, Don?"

Don just laughed. "No."

And laughed again.

We went inside, and the people were dressed like flowers in a garden—flowers in their hair, flowered skirts, flowered dresses, flowered shirts.

What were they all up to anyway?

We soon found out!

They were sending us to Hawaii!

We could not believe our church family had done this for us—and kept it a secret, too! We felt like the most loved people on earth.

We were excited! Never had we even imagined going on such a trip.

The accommodations were wonderful. Hawaii was even more beautiful than we imagined. We didn't want to waste any time while we were there. We were up at five, touring, walking, trying to see everything at once. We would go back to our room about seven or eight in the evening. While Hawaii partied, we got sleep so we could see more of the islands the next day. It was truly a wonderful vacation.

We flew to Maui for the last few days. Amid all the beauty, we sensed a serpent lurking in the garden. As we drove away from the tourist places, we began to see many people who had come through the sixties—the flower children, the hippies, now matured into converts of New Age teachings.

We drove along Hana Highway, going deep into the rain forest, trying to keep our eyes and car on the road with its hundreds of hairpin curves. At the same time, we were trying to see all of the cascading waterfalls. Some were so close, we could reach out our car window and touch them.

We saw a place to take a break from the dizzying ride. There, on the breathtaking mountain side overlooking the Pacific Ocean, was a trailer advertising snacks and cokes for sale. A young man with long, bushy, dark hair welcomed us, and we sat at the picnic table to talk with him. Daily we had prayed together for God's direction, and we led the conversation into our favorite subject, Jesus Christ.

"Don't tell me any more yet. I'll get my wife," Lani said.

"Martha!"

Martha and their children came to join us. She was a tall young woman with long blond hair, beautiful and friendly.

At that moment, we knew we had not come to this rain forest in Maui just to see the view. We knew in our hearts that God had arranged this whole trip for us to talk to Martha and Lani.

"Yoko Ono has been here! Lani was in the group that accompanied her as she searched for someone to channel the spirit of John Lennon!

Hmmm.

"Do you believe in reincarnation?" we asked.

"Oh, yes!"

"You know, Lani and Martha, many New Age leaders are saying that they lived thousands of years ago as a queen or a great warrior or a princess."

They nodded.

"And you believe them because they describe in detail lands they have never been to, societies they have never lived in, people they have never seen. Archeological discoveries later prove them right."

"That is why reincarnation has to be real," Martha said.

Lani and Martha were among the one out of four Americans who now believe in reincarnation, according to a poll conducted by George Gallup.

"The Bible has answers to all our questions," Paul went on. "We read in Hebrews 9:27... *it is appointed unto men once to die, but after this the judgment.'* Job 7:9- 10 says, *'As the cloud is consurned and vanisheth away; so he that goeth down to the grave shall come up no more. He shall return no more to his house, neither shall his place know him any more."*

"Jesus told us about two neighbors who died. One was a rich man and the other was a poor man named Lazarus. The rich man died and went immediately to hell where he pleaded that Lazarus return to earth to tell his brothers to avoid hell at all costs. Lazarus was carried by angels at his death to a place Jesus referred to as Abraham's bosom. The rich man's request was denied. There is no traveling back and forth after death, either as a spirit or in any other form. According to the Word of God, people do not live and die and live again in another person, animal, or even vegetable, as reincarnation teaches. Your New Age teachers are telling you there is a rebirth of the soul in successive bodies—a transmigration of souls—but God's Word teaches the opposite."

"You are taught that the purpose of reincarnation is so the soul will eventually receive release from the cycle of birth and death and regain its former pure state. But God tells us in the Bible *'He that is unjust, let him be unjust still; and he which is filthy, let him be filthy still; and he that is righteous, let him be righteous still: and he that is holy, let him be holy still.'* So... how does a person remember things and places and people from centuries ago? You need to understand, Lani and Martha, that souls do not transmigrate—but devils do!

"Devils?" they both asked at once.

"Jesus spent much of His ministry casting devils out of people. Devils are part of Satan's kingdom. They can inhabit a person. Jesus cast over six-thousand out of one man—and they transmigrated from the man into a herd of pigs. Then the pigs did what the devils try to cause people to do—about two-thousand pigs committed suicide by running violently down a steep bank and drowning themselves in the sea. Devils had left the man's body and entered into the bodies of animals."

"Jesus also told us about the unclean spirit that left a man and walked about seeking rest and found none. A spirit needs a body to work through. He was out looking for a body to inhabit. Unable to find one, he returned to the man he had left and found him still empty. He gathered together another seven spirits, more wicked than he was, and they all entered the man and lived in him, causing him to do things he never would have otherwise done."

There was a quietness at that picnic table in the rain forest of Maui that day. No cars drove in. Even the children were listening. (We learned later that Lani had locked the front gate!)

Martha said, "Do you know that we could take you to houses all over this island any evening for a walk-in?"

We thought she was changing the subject and imagined that a walk-in was probably someone who opened his home to anyone who wanted to walk in and talk. But neither assumption was true. Martha was not changing the subject and we were shocked when she explained to us what a walk-in was.

"A walk-in is where people get together and spirits walk in and out of them. They go on every night, all over this island."

No wonder we had sensed the serpent in the midst of this beauty!

"The spirits are the same demon spirits Jesus spoke about and cast out of people, Martha," Paul explained. "They have been around since the rebellion of Satan. And if one entered a person who lived today that had lived in a queen three-thousand years ago, that spirit would know all about the queen, her country, her people, her appearance, her society—everything. *People* do not come and go in different bodies—but the Bible clearly teaches that *devils* do!"

Martha sat thinking for a moment, then said, "So when people say they lived in another time and describe it they have a devil in them. It is really the devil who is describing someone he lived in earlier."

"That is exactly what happens, Martha," Paul said.

We then told them about Jesus, who came to set the captive free from devils that lead people into false teachings and a life of bondage, torment and misery. We spent hours with them.

Our visit ended with Lani and Martha praying to God for deliverance and salvation. Martha cried tears of repentance. When we left Martha was standing out by the road, tears streaming down her face, smiling and waving.

She called us a year later on her spiritual birthday, still serving Jesus, living now in California. Just recently, Martha called again. She is a little over two years old now in the Lord, still set free and loving Him and excited about serving Him.

What a Savior we have to introduce to people! There is no joy like leading a person to Jesus for salvation.

Of course, the devil was unhappy. In fact, he was enraged.

We came home to a church that felt just a little different from when we left. There was something in the air—and it wasn't the peace of the Lord.

We had left our youth pastor in charge while we were gone.

He and his new wife apparently liked the position more than the one they had.

He resigned and with a group that started out small, began a church less than a mile from ours. Telephones buzzed with lies being told about us and our church, and the group leaving grew larger.

We were heartbroken. We knew that there are good church splits and there are bad church splits, and we knew how to tell the difference between the two.

Down through the centuries, there have been times when a group of people had to leave churches that fell away from teaching the truth of God's Word. The Reformation, for example, led by Martin Luther, occurred because the Roman Catholic Church was teaching that a mere man was the head of the church, rather than the Biblical teaching that Jesus Christ alone heads His blood-bought church. There are groups of people today that are leaving churches that are condoning homosexuality and even ordaining men and women who have fallen into degraded lives of sin to be ministers in their denominations. When a church falls into apostasy, God's Word clearly commands us to turn away from it and come out from among such a people. When people leave a church for this reason, they leave praying for God to move upon the church they left, and give them back their first love and turn them back to the Word of God.

Then there are the bad splits. Unfortunately, there is no way for a soul-winning church to avoid them. We dwell in a fallen world and the enemy of men's souls is alive and at work to destroy the work of God. Heaven itself and God Himself endured an uprising. The devil drew one third of the angels of God to follow his leadership as he fought against God for His position. He was cast out of heaven... and he left lying.

Jesus said, "I am truth!"

Then He said of Satan, "There is no truth in him. He is a liar, and the father of it."

You've heard some of his lies. Evolution is one. Thomas Huxley, who gave his life to spreading Darwin's lie, said: "Evolution, if consistently accepted, makes it impossible to believe the Bible."

How many young people have turned away from the Bible and their Creator because of the lies Satan has spread against Him and His Word in our colleges and universities?

When a group of people leave a church lying, they have the mark of the first split upon them.

Satan also lied in the Garden of Eden.

"Ye shall not surely die," he said to Eve.

But she did.

And now we all do.

Oh, how lies hurt! They not only hurt the one being lied about, but they hurt the work of God. As lies spread throughout our town, we wondered how many we could have reached with the gospel would now never be saved. The things we heard about ourselves were amazing!

We heard that there was no anonymous giver who had made the large donation to our church. We heard that we ourselves gave the money out of our hordes in our Michigan savings accounts to keep from paying so much money in income taxes. The reason we gave, we heard, was so that others would give and the church would be paid for... so we could then sell it and skip town! *(No, we have no money stashed away. We still live by faith in the promises of God!)*

When that lie reached the ears of the donor, he came forward in front of the church one evening and identified himself. He gives to many ministries as God leads him, quietly, without wanting any recognition or praise for himself. But for our sake, he could no longer remain anonymous.

We heard that Paul owned the church (which he doesn't). It is deeded to the membership. We heard that we ourselves had planned our trip to Hawaii and were going there to start a church. Other vicious lies, with no truth in them, spread like fire through our area.

This split definitely had the mark of Satan upon it. And it hurt.

It is not so much those that spread the lies that hurt, but it crushed us when people we had considered true friends believed them. Why do these things happen in the church?

Paul warned the church of Ephesus, "...grievous wolves (shall) enter in among you, not sparing the flock. Also of your own selves shall men arise, speaking perverse things, to draw away disciples after them."

Perverse things... things that cause people to turn away from the right path.

The tragedy is that in every bad church split, there are people who leave, never to enter any church again.

Our prayer warriors kept right on praying. Alarms went off at every hour through the long nights, and people rose to cry out to God for His help.

One early morning in the midst of the raging storm, I had a dream.

I was standing in a large ship in a ferocious storm. Rugged sailors were frantically shouting orders and doing all the things they do to keep a boat from sinking. I saw people jumping overboard in terror and others tossed overboard by the gale. I saw one sailor run over to the front of the ship and jostle a man who was curled up sleeping under an overhanging board. Yes, it was Jesus. I saw the sailor talk to Him, then Jesus slowly and reluctantly stood to his feet. I could see he was exhausted.

He turned toward the sea, and said tiredly, "Peace. Be still."

The storm was history.

Jesus lay down and went back to sleep.

I woke up and thought about this dream. Then I prayed, "Lord, please wake up and tell this storm to become peace. There are people jumping overboard. Some are perishing in this storm. Even our church might perish in this storm!"

I felt His voice inside my spirit answer, "Why are you so worried about those who are leaving the ship? I am still in it! A ship can *never* sink while I am in it."

"Lord, thank you, thank you for staying in our ship. You're right. Our church will not go down, no matter how the storm rages, with you in the ship. But Lord. . . the disciples woke you up to get rid of the storm. Won't you please speak to the storm in our church and let peace return?"

"There is a time for everything. This is a time for a storm. I rebuked my disciples when they woke me up, for their lack of faith," he answered. "Have faith and remember... no ship will sink with me in it!

Have faith.

I'm supposed to be the one writing books about the subject. Where was mine when I needed it? Sometimes people come up to Paul and me and say, "Oh, you and Carolyn have so much faith."

It is true that faith begins small and grows as we realize we serve a prayer-answering God. But it is also true that we still need a fresh supply of faith for every need. Jesus had just given us the extra supply of faith we needed to make it through this storm.

"No ship will ever sink as long as I am in it."

And we didn't.

For two weeks, it looked like we were going down. The majority stood faithfully with us through the onslaught of lies, but it was tough on all of us.

And then beautiful new people started coming to church.

"God sent us here," they explained. "We drove by, and just kept feeling we should come in."

We had a new harvest of beautiful souls!

Our altars were filled with people seeking Christ as their Savior and Lord.

Our Bible Foundation Class was packed full of people, hungering for the Word of God.

We baptized new converts nearly every service.

We witnessed miracles of healing—incurable diseases vanishing without a trace, leaving doctors frustrated!

God was holding His church together even as the gates of hell itself raged against it. In the midst of it all, we knew that as long as the Presence of Jesus Christ remained in our church, we could keep sailing! God, not people, had called us to Foley. God, not people, would have to call us out. In the heat of the battle we would find ourselves rejoicing over a victory one minute and weeping with frustration and hurt the next. Slowly, the weeping times grew fewer and fewer, and we found our hours filled with rejoicing over victories in the lives of the new people God had brought to us.

One Saturday evening in December, our choir was singing at an outdoor pavilion in the State Park in Gulf Shores, Alabama. It was a miserable night, cold and wet. A few people from the park huddled against the buildings, listening and trying in vain to keep dry at the same time. After the concert, we were packing up our equipment to leave when the man who had given the stocks approached Paul. We had not even seen him there.

"You're for real, aren't you?"

"What do you mean?"

"Well, anyone who would stand out here singing on a miserable night like this just to win one more soul to Christ must be for real."

Then he added this line that made the evening much less miserable.

"I'm going to pay off your church."

We hadn't quit praying.

Stocks were transferred again.

Another donation, this time of over $111,000!

It seems incredible yet, as I write this huge amount! We are so thankful to our prayer-answering Father! And we are so very thankful for His generous servant!

We had only $16,000 more to pray in!

With no begging or even passing an offering plate, the $16,000 was paid by the rest of the congregation in just two Sundays.

In just over five years, we had paid over $430,000 on our mortgage. We were now debt free!

You may ask, "Are you bragging?"

Yes, we are. We are bragging about our God and His power to do anything He decides to do for His children. We read in the sixteenth chapter of I Chronicles:

Remember his marvellous works that he hath done, his wonders!

Declare his marvellous works among all nations!

O give thanks unto the Lord; for he is good; for his mercy endureth for ever!

We rode out the storm, and our church was strengthened by the experience. Someone said, "Smooth sailing does not make strong sailors."

We all dread going through storms, but they do force us into becoming stronger sailors!

Some precious people who had left have come back to worship with us. What a reunion we had!

One precious sixteen year old boy was caught up in the split. We were no longer able to work with him. Two years later, he lay in a coffin, the result of a car accident. We hope to see him in heaven. The bad church splits always include tragic results.

We personally know many pastors whose ministries were ruined as a result of the havoc and devastation caused by the lies and cruelty of people leaving a church.

We thank our Lord, our faithful Captain, who skillfully brought our tossing ship through the storm.

Without Jesus, we would have sunk.

3

The harvest truly is plenteous, but the labourers are few; pray ye therefore the Lord of the harvest, that he will send forth labourers into his harvest.
(Matthew 9:37-38)

*W*e set aside the entire month of September as *Harvest Month.* We promised our people that we would devote every service—Sunday School classes, Pioneer Club meetings, youth meetings, concerts, every time we met—to winning souls. One new Christian, who has had nearly nothing but raging storms in her life, cried out to God for her family to be saved during *Harvest Month.*

She brought her brother, who was gloriously saved and baptized. Then the last Sunday of September came ...and Deborah's sister, son, daughter-in-law, grandchildren and sister's children came to church.

Her son and daughter-in-law wept their way to Jesus at the altar on Sunday morning. Sunday evening they were baptized and, with tears streaming down their faces, told the congregation of their brand new beginning in life. They had us all weeping!

I asked, "Deborah, how did you get your family to come to church?"

She answered, "When I heard about *Harvest Month*, I decided to do all I could to see my family saved. For the past three weeks, I have served my family. I have done the laundry, taken care of the children, scrubbed and cleaned, baked and cooked. When they thanked me, I told them not to thank me, but to thank my Jesus. I was doing it for Him, so He was really the One who was doing things for them. . . because He wants them to love Him like I do."

Her labor of love reaped her harvest. We can long for and pray for the salvation of our loved ones, but faith without works is dead, being alone. If all Christians in this sin-sick world could just add works to our faith, what a harvest of souls we could see!

Our son-in-law, Jim, Elizabeth's husband, went to Florida to harvest his vending machines of quarters, and harvested two souls while there! God placed a destitute man in his path whose home was the streets of Daytona Beach. Jim won him to Christ in the parking lot of *Popeye's Restaurant*.

They were praising their Savior together, when Jim said, "Charlie, it's Wednesday evening. There is a church near here, and we need to go."

Charlie looked horrified at the thought.

"Look at me, Jim. I'm filthy. My hair is greasy. My clothes are dirty and worn. I can't go to church looking like this!"

"It doesn't matter how you're dressed, Charlie. God doesn't care and real people of God don't care either. Let's go to church so you will have a church family here to help you, because I'm going back to my family in Alabama."

Charlie was unconvinced.

"I just can't go into a church looking like this, Jim. I can't."

"I'll tell you what, Charlie. We'll go into *Popeye's Restaurant*. We're about the same size. You can have my clothes. I'll wear yours, and we'll go to church together."

"You would do that... for me?"

"I surely would. Come on."

"No. If you would do that for me, I'll go like I am. It's okay. Let's go to church. "

They couldn't find a church open in the area, but Jim broke down and wept as he was relating this story to us. "It would have been an honor to wear his filthy clothes for my Jesus," he said.

Our Savior exchanged His beautiful, clean garments for our filthy, stained ones. He left the splendor of His golden heaven, and came down to a fallen world to get a people to take back home with Him.

"But I can't go to heaven dressed like this! I'm filthy!"

So He takes our filth, our sins upon Himself. Then He dresses us in His beautiful snow-white garment of righteousness.

He puts His arm around us and says, "Come on. You're ready now. Let's go see our Father."

Have you given Him your filthy garments of sin? Have you let Him dress you in His sparkling white robes of righteousness?

The exchange all takes place at the foot of the old rugged cross.

What a Savior. Truly, He is the Pearl of great price. This world with all its wealth pales into insignificance when compared to our precious Jesus. As long as He sails with us through the storms of life, why would any of us even think of leaving the boat?

We have come a little farther now by faith....

He has never forsaken us. He catches us when we stumble, to keep us from falling. He reminds us of His Presence when our friends forsake us.

He lights our way during the dark times of life.

He is still our closest Friend, who keeps His promise to stick to us closer than a brother.

He is no respecter of persons. We have met countless people who have placed their hand in His and have been led down their path of faith. He has gently taken care of each one.

If you have never received Him as your Savior and Lord, place your hand in His today. On that glorious day when we all gather around His throne, you will sing with the rest of us:

We've come this far by faith,
Leaning on the Lord
Trusting in His holy Word
He's never failed us yet.

A SHOCKING TESTIMONY
FROM ONE OF OUR READERS

A beautiful young couple entered our church in February, 1997. We gave them this book, so they could become acquainted with us and with our ministry.

Tammy has her own home day care, and cares for six children under three years old. She began reading *We've Come This Far By Faith.* In spite of not having time to even read one page at once, she was determined to finish the book—one sentence at a time, one or two minutes at a time. Almost immediately she was afflicted physically with burning aches and pains. Three year old Hannah and her two year old brother, concerned to see their caregiver near tears, laid their tiny hands on her back and prayed for Jesus to heal her. They continued to do this each time they saw her gripped with pain, and she continued working and reading during that week through answers to their prayers alone. The doctor confined her to bed during the weekend and prescribed strong pain medication. She decided to omit the medication and read instead. Her body continued to be racked with pain. It was Wednesday when she read page 233 and the paragraph that changed her life. You may be surprised which one spoke to her heart....

Paul and Roy hurried to the city park, and Paul noticed four crosses and in front of them a circle. A man in a white robe and women in black robes with black eye masks and hoods stood in front of them. Then the circle and the crosses were set a flame.

There were two women in black robes with black eye masks that day who set fire to the crosses. Tammy was one of them. She was twenty years old at the time, and it was implied that her job would be in jeopardy if she did not comply with this order. She questioned the assignment given her, but was told that a cross burning was neither racial nor Satanic. "We've been doing this for years," she was told by her superiors. She buried her uncomfortable feeling inside, and obeyed orders in order to keep her job.

Tammy read that paragraph over and over again, each time seeing herself and her act that day in the park. Finally she read on, and horror gripped her heart as she realized for the first time what she had done against the Savior she professed to love and serve. She suddenly realized that she had not only hurt Him, but also had invited the presence of Satan into her life by her deed.

She began to understand for the first time why so many things had happened in her life after setting fire to the cross. Oppression by the enemy had enveloped her and her home. Shortly after burning the crosses, she moved to a house that was near a little abandoned church. While feeding and rocking her small children in the middle of the night, she often noticed lights on in the church. She wondered who was in the building, as it was no longer used for church services.

She felt surrounded by evil, and often, day and night, she would see someone near her out of the corner of her eye. She would turn quickly, only to have the presence disappear. One day, she heard a strange sound in her son's room while he was sleeping. That was the day she came face to face with a devil. Tammy describes him as the ugliest being human eyes could ever see. He was holding her son in his arms and told her he was going to sacrifice him to the devil at the church next door. Tammy, shy by nature, suddenly found herself demanding the demon to put her child down, in the name of Jesus. She does not know how long she continued to resist the devil and rebuke his plan, but finally she saw the hand of God reach out, take her baby, and lay him gently back into his crib. The demon simply faded away. She later learned that the building was being used by Satanists.

Tammy often began to tell someone about her encounter with the demon, but would suddenly stop and tell her listener she would finish the story later. Each time she spoke of her experience, she would spend a sleepless night tossing with nightmares and a gripping fear for her son. She remained in bondage to these fears and this darkness in her life—until she found herself in this book.

She confessed her sin to God and asked for His cleansing by the blood of Jesus. God, as always in reply to sincere hearts, drove out evil and darkness with the Light and beauty of Jesus Christ.

Tammy says, "To God be the glory! I no longer have nightmares! Fear no longer grips my heart when my son is out of my sight! I have been delivered and set free from the torment of Satan! I believe my son will be used by God!"

Tammy's testimony has both a warning and victory in its message. Gods Word says, *"Neither give place to the devil"* (Ephesians 4:27). Heed this warning carefully, dear Friend. One action by Tammy at the age of twenty brought years of heartache into her life. God would have provided for her needs if she had obeyed His still small voice of warning! God's provision is not limited to a person's job! Stand for Jesus Christ, no matter what the cost! Never... *never*... give the devil an invitation into your life! If you are oppressed, as Tammy was for so many years, by darkness, depression and evil, look back into your life to see if you have committed sins that you have not repented of. God's Word says, *"If we confess our sins, he is faithful and just to forgive us our sins, and to cleanse us from all unrighteousness"* (I John 1:9).

So many believe they have obeyed this commandment by merely telling God that they are sinners. But God tells us to confess **our sins!** We are to name them! With admission of each sin comes not only forgiveness, but also cleansing and deliverance! If you have been involved with astrology, pornography, ouija boards, fortune tellers, fornication, adultery, witchcraft, rebellion, hatred, drugs or any of the things that are part of Satan's kingdom, confess (admit) each sin to God. When we have done our part by confessing, God will then be faithful to do His part and forgive and cleanse us from evil.

Tammy's testimony is also one of victory. Jesus had again done what He said He came to do: to set captives free by bringing liberty to those in bondage!

Jesus said, *"Him that cometh to me I will in no wise cast out"* (John 6:37). He who is Truth, cannot lie! If you come to Him, He promised He would not cast you out, but will keep His Word. His invitation is, *"Come unto me, all ye that labour and are heavy laden, and I will give you rest"* (Matthew 11:28).

He will do for you what He did for Tammy! He *will* forgive you! He *will* cleanse you! He *will* deliver you from evil! (Incidentally, the four words, *"Deliver us from evil"* are removed from the Lord's prayer in many of the new Bible translations. Satan, the thief, has stolen them, for he does not want anyone asking God for deliverance from evil!) When Tammy began reading this book, Satan knew she would discover the reasons for the torment that filled her life. He afflicted her to the point of being bedridden. But she persisted and gained the victory! And you can too, so you can join Tammy in proclaiming, "To God be the Glory!"

Tammy and her beautiful family are now members of our church family. It is a special thrill to hear the one who once burned the crosses sing sweet praises to our Lord!

Paul and Carolyn

Paul and his saxophone

New Life In Christ Church • Foley, Alabama

A look inside New Life in Christ Church

Paul and Carolyn Wilde have written the book, **"Seven Biblical Principles For Financial Peace of Mind."** They have learned through their walk of faith that there are seven principles we must follow as Christians if we want the blessing of God upon our lives.

Some people follow two or three of them, and then wonder why God's blessings are not upon them. We as Christians, especially in the coming days of financial turmoil and economic collapse of the monetary system as we know it, need to know and put into practice *every single one* of these principles.

As our world grows blacker and hatred against Christ and His followers intensifies, we believe that all Christians will be called upon to live by faith. The book you have just read has shown you that we serve a God who is always faithful to His own. If God took care of Paul and Carolyn and their eight children, He will surely take care of you. But there are principles you must adhere to in this new way of life. And you need to begin now!

"Seven Biblical Principles For Financial Peace of Mind" will show you the principles Christians must live by to enter into this new relationship with God of walking by total faith in Him, and Him alone.

If you have enjoyed
WE'VE COME THIS FAR BY FAITH
you are sure to enjoy Carolyn's new book,
TORCHBEARERS

Torchbearers is more than a novel. Woven in with the fictional characters are 37 thrilling biographies of men, women and teenagers who have carried the torch for Christ.

Dave, a fictional character, is an Olympic champion runner. God calls Dave to run in His race. This Christian race is depicted as a relay race that has been going on since New Testament times. Receiving the torch and carrying it to the next runner are torchbearers from every century. As Dave faces challenges and hardships and meets people who need encouragement, he receives and gives inspiration by remembering the lives of torchbearers of the past who have faced similar tough situations and emerged conquerors. The torchbearers chosen include people we can all relate to—ordinary people who have faced the same fears and situations that we confront today.

Read what they are saying....

"One of the best books I have ever read in my lifetime... my life and ministry has not been the same!"

Dwight L Kinman, Author & Conference Speaker

"I have shared many passages from Torchbearers with my friends and family. I could not put it down! I recommend this book to any person carrying the torch for Jesus who has ever felt alone, rejected, or just in need of little encouragement."

Rosey Bryan, Wife of Andy, Southern Baptist Evangelist

"...a challenging message and a sharply painted picture of our rich Christian heritage."

Gulf Coast Christian Newspaper

"I was totally awe-stricken! The encouragement one can receive from reading this book is much needed."

Quinton Mills, Evangelist, Songwriter

291